Gooseberry Patch co.

A Country Store In Your Mailbox®

Christmas Pantry

A Country Store In Your Mailbox®

Gooseberry Patch
600 London Road
Department Book
Delaware, OH 43015

★

1-800-854-6673
gooseberrypatch.com

Copyright 2000, Gooseberry Patch 1-888052-74-0
Fourth Printing, May, 2002

How To Subscribe

Would you like to receive
"A Country Store in Your Mailbox"®?
For a 2-year subscription to our 96-page
Gooseberry Patch catalog, simply send $3.00 to:

Gooseberry Patch
600 London Road
Delaware, OH 43015

Contents

Dedication

For everyone who loves
stringing popcorn, winter hayrides,
rosy cheeks & homemade cocoa
on a frosty night.

Appreciation

Thanks to all who shared
their treasured favorites for making
this an old-fashioned Christmas.

Frosty Mornings

Gingerbread Waffles

Jill Valentine
Jackson, TN

*A family favorite, this spicy blend of cinnamon and molasses
is great for a frosty winter morning!*

2 c. all-purpose flour
1-1/2 t. baking powder
3/4 t. baking soda
1/2 t. salt
2 T. sugar
1 t. ginger

1/2 t. cinnamon
1/4 t. cloves
2 eggs
1/4 c. oil
1/3 c. molasses
1-1/2 c. buttermilk

Combine flour, baking powder, baking soda, salt, sugar, ginger, cinnamon and cloves in a large mixing bowl. In a separate bowl, mix together eggs, oil, molasses and buttermilk. Make a well in the center of the flour mixture and pour buttermilk mixture in; blend until thoroughly combined. Bake waffles in preheated greased waffle iron. Makes 5 to 6 waffles.

*Bring old-fashioned charm to your kitchen.
Use strands of raffia to tie sprigs of boxwood
to vintage cookie jars, antique sifters, tin sugar
shakers, apothecary jars and milk bottles.*

Marmalade French Toast

Jo Ann

This is the perfect breakfast dish to serve to your out-of-town guests!

8-oz. pkg. cream cheese,
   softened
1-1/2 t. vanilla extract, divided
1/2 c. walnuts, finely chopped
1 French bread loaf, thickly
   sliced

4 eggs
1 c. whipping cream
1/2 t. nutmeg
12-oz. jar orange marmalade
1/2 c. orange juice

Blend together cream cheese and one teaspoon vanilla; fold in nuts
and set aside. Using a sharp knife, cut a pocket in the top of each
bread slice. Spoon 2 tablespoons of cream cheese mixture into the
pocket of each bread slice. Combine eggs, cream, nutmeg and
remaining vanilla; place in a large, shallow bowl. Carefully dip bread
in egg mixture and cook on a lightly oiled griddle until golden; flip and
cook on second side. Place bread on an ungreased baking sheet and
bake at 300 degrees for 20 minutes. Mix marmalade and orange juice
in a small saucepan; heat through. Drizzle over hot French toast.
Makes about 8 servings.

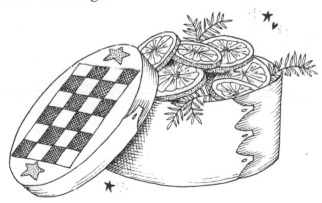

The fireside is the tulip bed of a winter day.

-Persian Proverb

Country Crunch Pancakes

Kathy Grashoff
Ft. Wayne, IN

A favorite recipe that was shared with me by an Amish friend in our community. The crunchy topping makes these terrific!

2 c. all-purpose flour
1/3 c. whole-wheat flour
1/2 c. plus 1/3 c. quick-cooking
   oatmeal, divided
2 T. sugar
2 t. baking powder
1 t. baking soda

1 t. salt
2 t. cinnamon, divided
2-1/4 c. buttermilk
2 eggs, beaten
2 T. oil
1 c. blueberries
1/4 c. chopped almonds
1/4 c. brown sugar, packed

In a mixing bowl, combine flours, 1/3 cup oatmeal, sugar, baking powder, baking soda, salt and one teaspoon cinnamon. In a separate bowl, combine buttermilk, eggs and oil. Stir into dry ingredients until blended; fold in blueberries. Mix together remaining oatmeal and cinnamon. Blend in almonds and brown sugar. Sprinkle about one teaspoon topping for each pancake onto a lightly greased hot griddle. Pour 1/4 cup batter over topping. Immediately sprinkle with another teaspoonful of topping. Turn when bubbles form on top of pancakes. Cook until second side is golden brown.

Tuck votives in the cups of muffin tins, tiny tart pans, terra cotta pots or custard cups. Surround them with rosehips or one-inch cinnamon sticks for a spicy fragrance.

Frosty Mornings

Christmas Morning Rolls ✓⭐

Charlotte Varner
West Point, VA

Best served with an icy glass of milk!

24 frozen dinner rolls
3-3/4 oz. pkg. non-instant
   butterscotch pudding mix
1/2 c. butter

3/4 c. brown sugar, packed
1/2 c. chopped walnuts
3/4 t. cinnamon

Arrange frozen rolls in greased tube pan. Sprinkle dry pudding mix over rolls. Cook butter, brown sugar, walnuts and cinnamon over low heat until sugar is dissolved and mixture bubbles; pour over rolls. Cover tightly with foil and let stand on counter overnight. Bake, uncovered, at 350 degrees for 30 minutes. Let stand 5 minutes, then invert onto serving platter.

Overnight Sour Cream Coffee Cake ⭐

Nancy McDonald
Valrico, FL

Great served with fruit and freshly-brewed, flavored coffee on a breakfast buffet.

3/4 c. butter, softened
1 c. sugar
2 eggs
8 oz. sour cream
2 c. all-purpose flour
1 t. baking powder

1 t. baking soda
1/2 t. salt
1 t. nutmeg
3/4 c. brown sugar, packed
1 t. cinnamon
1/2 c. chopped pecans

Cream butter and sugar together until light and fluffy. Add eggs and sour cream until well mixed. Combine next 5 ingredients. Add to batter and mix well. Pour into greased and floured 13"x9" pan. In a separate bowl, mix brown sugar, cinnamon and pecans; sprinkle evenly over batter. Cover and refrigerate overnight. Uncover and bake at 350 degrees for 35 to 40 minutes. Makes 15 servings.

Orange-Nut Muffins

Brenda Hurst
Greenwood, IN

*For a quick breakfast treat, bake in mini muffin tins
and serve with a slice of quiche!*

3-oz. pkg. cream cheese,
   softened
1 c. sugar
2 t. vanilla extract
1 egg
2 c. all-purpose flour
1 t. baking soda
1 t. salt

1/2 c. sour cream
2 11-oz. cans mandarin
   oranges, drained and
   chopped
3 T. orange zest, divided
1/2 c. pecans, finely chopped
3 T. orange juice
2 c. powdered sugar

In a large bowl, beat cream cheese, sugar and vanilla until smooth.
Beat in egg for one to 2 minutes. In separate bowl, combine flour,
baking soda and salt. Add flour mixture and sour cream alternately
into cream cheese mixture, blending on low. Fold in oranges, one
tablespoon orange zest and nuts. Pour into lined muffin tins. Bake at
375 degrees for 15 to 20 minutes; let cool. Combine orange juice,
powdered sugar and remaining orange zest; blend well and drizzle
over muffins.

*Frost the glass panes
in an old wooden
window frame with snow
spray, then write fun
messages in the "snow."
Hang it on your porch
to greet guests!*

Frosty Mornings

Grandma's Waffles

Cecelia Grossman
Omaha, NE

I think this recipe makes the best waffles! One of my fondest memories was of staying with my grandparents and enjoying Grandma Cosgrove's waffles in the morning.

3 c. milk
3 eggs, beaten
8 T. butter, melted
3 T. sugar

2 t. vanilla extract
3 c. all-purpose flour
3 t. baking powder

Blend together milk and eggs. Add butter and sugar; stir in vanilla. Combine dry ingredients and add to the milk mixture. Heat waffle iron and brush with oil. Pour in enough batter to fill waffle iron, close and bake until steaming stops and waffles are crisp and golden.

Make a quick country gift...fill a glass canning jar with cranberries and sprigs of boxwood or a selection of old buttons and spools. A glass votive holder will rest inside the jar rim; just tuck a tealight inside!

French Banana Pancakes

Calico Inn
Sevierville, TN

A delicious way to serve pancakes!

1 c. all-purpose flour
1/4 c. powdered sugar
2 eggs, beaten
1 c. milk
1/4 c. plus 3 T. butter, melted
   and divided
1 t. vanilla extract
1/4 t. salt

1/4 c. brown sugar, packed
1/4 t. cinnamon
1/4 t. nutmeg
1/4 c. whipping cream
5 to 6 bananas, halved
   lengthwise
Garnish: whipping cream,
   whipped and cinnamon

Stir flour and powdered sugar into a mixing bowl; add eggs, milk,
3 tablespoons butter, vanilla and salt; beat until smooth. Heat a lightly
greased 6" skillet; add 3 tablespoons batter, spreading to almost cover
bottom of skillet. Cook until lightly browned; turn and brown the other
side. Remove to a wire rack; repeat with remaining batter. To prepare
filling, melt 1/4 cup butter in a large skillet, then stir in brown sugar,
cinnamon and nutmeg. Blend in cream and cook over low heat until
slightly thickened, then add half of the bananas to skillet. Heat for
2 to 3 minutes, spooning sauce over bananas; remove bananas and
set aside; repeat with remaining bananas. Roll a pancake around each
banana half and place on a serving platter, spoon sauce over the
pancakes. Top with whipped cream and cinnamon. Makes 10 to
12 pancakes.

I am in holiday humor!

-William Shakespeare

Frosty Mornings

Cinnamon Rolls

Kathy Grashoff
Ft. Wayne, IN

I'd never made cinnamon rolls because you always had to knead the dough and it seemed like a lot of work. Then I found this recipe; it's so simple and delicious!

2 sticks margarine
1 c. sugar
1 c. boiling water
2 pkgs. active dry yeast
1 c. warm water
1 egg

5 to 7 c. all-purpose flour
1 stick margarine, melted and
    divided
1/3 c. brown sugar, packed and
    divided
cinnamon to taste

In a large bowl, blend together 2 sticks margarine, sugar and boiling water. Dissolve yeast in warm water, add egg and whisk with a fork; stir into margarine mixture. Add flour, a little at a time, until dough cleans the sides of the bowl. Cover bowl with towel and let rise until double. Roll out 1/2 of the dough to a 12"x8" rectangle; spread with 1/2 stick melted margarine. Sprinkle on half the brown sugar and cinnamon. Beginning with the long end, roll up, jelly roll-style and slice with serrated knife into 12 rolls. Repeat with the remaining half of dough. Place on greased cookie sheet, leaving about one inch between each roll. Cover with towel and let double in size. Bake at 350 degrees for 15 to 20 minutes. When cool, frost with your favorite icing if desired. Makes about 2 dozen.

Stuff a mitten or stocking with fresh greenery, holly, princess pine and mistletoe. Add a wire hanger then slip over a neighbor's door knob for a holiday surprise!

Yummy Apple Muffins

Ruth Palmer
Glendale, UT

Since we have apple trees, this is one of our family favorites. They're great at Christmas as gifts for friends and neighbors; just place them in a plastic bag and tie with a holiday bow.

1 c. sugar
2 c. all-purpose flour
1 t. nutmeg
2 t. cinnamon
2 t. baking powder
2 t. baking soda

2 eggs
1/2 c. oil
5 c. apples, peeled, cored and
   coarsely chopped
1 c. chopped walnuts
1/2 c. raisins

Sift together first 6 ingredients. In a separate bowl, whisk eggs and oil, fold in apples, walnuts and raisins; add to dry ingredients. Spoon into greased muffin tins and bake at 350 degrees for 20 minutes or until done. Makes 2 dozen muffins.

A merry Christmas to everybody!
A happy New Year to all the world!

-Charles Dickens

Raspberry French Toast

Joanne Anderson
Scottsdale, AZ

Don't miss any of the fun Christmas morning! After you get the kids to bed Christmas Eve, just spend a few minutes preparing this recipe, refrigerate then bake in the morning.

12 white bread slices, crusts trimmed, cubed and divided
2 8-oz. pkgs. cream cheese, cubed
2 c. raspberries, divided
12 eggs, beaten

2 c. milk
1/3 c. maple syrup or honey
1 c. sugar
2 T. cornstarch
1 c. water
1 T. butter

Place half the bread cubes into a greased 13"x9" baking dish. Place cream cheese over the bread, top with one cup berries and remaining bread. In a large bowl, blend together eggs, milk and syrup or honey; mix well. Pour over bread mixture, cover and chill for 8 hours or overnight. Remove from refrigerator 30 minutes before baking. Cover and bake at 350 degrees for 30 minutes. Uncover; bake 25 to 30 minutes longer or until golden brown and the center is set. In a saucepan, combine sugar and cornstarch; add water. Bring to a boil over medium heat; boil for 3 minutes, stirring constantly. Stir in remaining berries; reduce heat. Stir in butter until melted. Serve over French toast. Makes 6 to 8 servings.

Homemade jams and jellies are always welcome and make yummy holiday gifts! Wrap the jars with raffia then glue an old-fashioned yo-yo on the bow; top the yo-yo with a vintage button!

Cinnamon Roll Pancakes

Robyn Schellhorn
Greenwood Village, CO

These are so quick and easy to make!

1-1/2 c. milk
1 t. cinnamon
1 t. nutmeg

2 eggs
2 lg. prebaked cinnamon rolls

Beat milk, spices and eggs together in a shallow bowl. Slice cinnamon rolls in half horizontally and dip in mixture, coating well. Cook over medium heat on a lightly oiled griddle or in a skillet until golden brown.

Cinnamon Cream Syrup:

1 c. sugar
1/2 c. corn syrup
1/4 c. water

1/2 to 3/4 t. cinnamon
1/2 c. evaporated milk

Combine sugar, corn syrup, water and cinnamon in saucepan. Bring to a boil over medium heat, stirring constantly. Cook and stir for 2 minutes longer. Remove from heat and cool for 5 minutes; stir in milk. Serve over cinnamon roll pancakes. Makes 1-2/3 cups.

For a camp-style welcome, fill sap buckets with your favorite wintertime decorations...twigs, evergreens, apples, pomegranates, holly and mistletoe!

Frosty Mornings

Mom's Muffin Doughnuts

Lori Doss
Apple Valley, CA

*Mom made these for us when we were kids...they always
smelled so good and tasted even better!*

2 c. all-purpose flour
3 t. baking powder
1/2 t. salt
1/2 t. nutmeg
1-1/2 T. shortening
1/2 c. sugar

2 eggs
1/2 c. milk
1/2 c. chopped walnuts
1/2 c. butter, melted
1 c. cinnamon-sugar

Sift together first 4 ingredients; set aside. In a large bowl, cream
shortening with sugar and add eggs; beat well. Stir in dry ingredients,
milk and walnuts. Pour batter into a muffin tin lined with paper
muffin cups. Bake at 400 degrees for 20 minutes. Let cool slightly,
then remove muffins from paper cups. Dip in butter and roll in
cinnamon-sugar. Makes 16 doughnuts.

*Make a snowman kit
for your favorite kids!
Just fill a decorated
box with lots of flea
market finds...a hat,
large buttons, a flannel
scarf, mittens, twigs and
an old corncob pipe.
All the kids have to add
is snow and a carrot nose!*

Cheesy Holiday Eggs

Melanie Heffner
Beaverton, OR

I especially like these served with fresh fruit
and muffins or coffee cake.

12 t. half-and-half
12 eggs
pepper to taste

12 T. Cheddar cheese, shredded
6 t. fresh Parmesan cheese,
   grated

Spray a 12-cup muffin pan or 12 custard cups with non-stick spray. Place one teaspoon half-and-half in the bottom of each pan or cup then break an egg into each. With kitchen food scissors, cut cross-wise through each egg yolk; sprinkle with pepper. Top each egg with one tablespoon Cheddar cheese and 1/2 teaspoon Parmesan cheese. Bake at 350 degrees for 15 minutes. Loosen eggs with rubber spatula and slide onto a warmed plate.

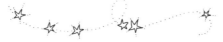

Cinnamon-Apple Oatmeal

Kirsten Housand
Elkhart, IN

Tasty with brown sugar and milk poured over the top.

1/2 c. applesauce
3/4 c. sugar
2 eggs
3 c. quick-cooking oatmeal
2 t. baking powder

1/2 t. salt
1/2 t. cinnamon
1 c. milk
1 c. apples, peeled, cored and
   chopped

Combine applesauce, sugar and eggs with mixer until well blended. Add next 5 ingredients and beat well. Fold in apples and pour into a greased 8"x8" pan. Bake at 400 degrees for 30 minutes.

Hang a kissing ball in your doorway...whoever is caught standing under it must get a kiss!

Frosty Mornings

Blueberry Surprise French Toast

Pamela Jaeger
Farmington, MI

This is one of those wonderful overnight recipes...just pull it out of the refrigerator Christmas morning and let it bake while your family begins to open their presents; nothing could be easier!

1 c. brown sugar, packed
1/2 c. butter
2 T. corn syrup
1 c. chopped pecans
8 to 10 c. Italian bread, cubed
    and divided
2 oz. cream cheese
3 c. blueberries

1 c. sugar
1 t. cinnamon
1/2 t. nutmeg
6 eggs
2 c. milk
1 t. vanilla extract
1/4 t. salt

Combine brown sugar, butter and corn syrup in a small saucepan. Cook over medium heat until thickened, stirring constantly. Pour into a 13"x9" baking dish; sprinkle pecans over the syrup. Place half of the bread cubes evenly over the mixture in the pan. Slice the cream cheese into 4 thin slices. Cut each one in half lengthwise, then cube. Arrange these over the bread; sprinkle on berries. Mix sugar, cinnamon and nutmeg together, sprinkle over berries; top with remaining bread cubes. Beat together eggs, milk, vanilla and salt. Pour evenly over whole dish, making sure to moisten bread. Do not stir. Cover and refrigerate for 7 hours or overnight. Take the dish out of the refrigerator about 30 minutes before baking. Bake, uncovered, at 350 degrees for one hour or until lightly browned. Let stand 15 to 20 minutes or until firm, then turn upside down onto serving platter and cut into squares.

The more the merrier!

-John Heywood

Santa Face Pancakes

Susan Young
Madison, AL

In the late 1940's my father made these for breakfast on Christmas morn'. Served with whipped cream, we always had great fun making Santa's beard!

6 bacon slices, cut into fourths
   and cooked
1-1/4 c. all-purpose flour
3 t. baking powder
1/2 t. salt
2 T. sugar

1 egg
2 T. oil
3/4 to 1 c. milk
Garnish: strawberry syrup and
   whipped cream

Prepare bacon; set aside. Sift dry ingredients into a large bowl. Make a well in the center and add egg, oil and 3/4 cup milk. Quickly stir until just blended; batter should not be thin. Add more milk if needed. When griddle is hot, pour 1/4 cup batter per pancake onto griddle. As each pancake is poured, place pieces of bacon to resemble, eyes, nose and mouth. When surface edges bubble, turn pancake over. Continue cooking until golden brown. Serve with strawberry syrup for Santa's hat and whipped cream for his beard.

Give a loaf of your favorite sweet bread tucked inside a stocking or oven mitt! Wrap the loaf securely in plastic wrap then tuck inside. Miniature loaves also make wonderful mitten stuffers.

Frosty Mornings

Maple-Pecan Casserole

Sharon Shepherd
Terre Haute, IN

The raisin bread in this recipe makes it extra special!

8-oz. pkg. fully cooked sausage
   patties
16-oz. pkg. raisin bread, cubed
6 eggs, beaten
1-1/2 c. milk
1-1/2 c. half-and-half
1 t. vanilla extract

1/4 t. nutmeg
1/4 t. cinnamon
1 c. brown sugar, packed
1 c. chopped pecans
1/2 c. butter
2 T. maple syrup

Brown sausage, drain fat and cut into bite-size pieces. Place bread cubes in an oiled 13"x9" baking dish; top with sausage. Combine eggs, milk, half-and-half, vanilla, nutmeg and cinnamon and pour over bread and sausage. Cover and refrigerate 8 hours or overnight. In a bowl, mix brown sugar, pecans, butter and maple syrup. Drop by teaspoonfuls over egg mixture. Bake at 350 degrees for 35 to 40 minutes.

Give the kids' teachers an A+! Melt white chocolate in a double boiler then use a small brush to paint an "A+" on several bright red apples. Place them in a basket for a fun holiday gift!

Blueberry Cream Muffins

Linda Hensz
Damascus, PA

*Every summer we pick an abundance of wild blueberries and I
always freeze some to enjoy later in these delicious muffins.*

4 eggs	1 t. salt
2 c. sugar	1 t. baking soda
1 c. oil	2 t. baking powder
1 t. vanilla extract	2 c. sour cream
4 c. all-purpose flour	2 c. blueberries

Beat eggs then gradually add sugar, while beating. Slowly add oil
and vanilla. Combine dry ingredients and add alternately with sour
cream to the egg mixture. Gently fold in blueberries. Spoon into
greased muffin tins. Bake at 400 degrees for 20 minutes. Makes
2 dozen muffins.

Alaska Pancakes

Jean-Marie Longmore
Las Cruces, NM

Mom shared this recipe with me when I was a new bride.

1/3 c. warm water	1/2 c. milk
1 pkg. active dry yeast	1 egg
1 c. biscuit baking mix	

Blend together water and yeast; stir until dissolved. Add biscuit mix,
milk and egg; beating until smooth. For each pancake, spoon about
1/4 cup of batter onto hot griddle. When the batter begins to bubble,
turn and cook until golden. Makes about one dozen pancakes.

*Christmas; that magic blanket
that wraps itself about us.*

-Augusta E. Rundel

Frosty Mornings

Cinnamon Streusel Coffee Cake ✓

Sally Kelly
Akron, OH

Of all the recipes Mom made while my sister and I were growing up, this one became a family favorite.

3 c. plus 4 T. all-purpose flour, divided
6 t. baking powder
1/2 t. salt
1-1/2 c. sugar
1/2 c. margarine
2 eggs, beaten

1 c. milk
2 t. vanilla extract
1 c. brown sugar, packed
4 t. cinnamon
4 T. margarine, melted and cooled

Mix 3 cups flour, baking powder, salt and sugar. Cut in margarine until mixture resembles cornmeal. Blend in eggs, milk and vanilla. Stir just enough to thoroughly combine. Pour into a greased and floured 13"x9" pan and spread evenly. Mix brown sugar, remaining flour, cinnamon and melted margarine. Sprinkle topping over batter and bake at 375 degrees for 25 to 30 minutes.

Wrap a glass votive with cinnamon sticks or magnolia leaves; secure them with a rubber band. Hide the rubber band with strands of raffia, a strip of homespun or a length of copper wire.

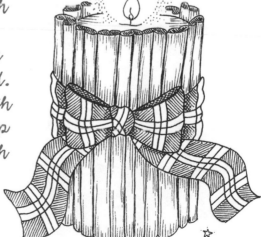

Brunch Egg Squares

Gloria Kaufmann
Orrville, OH

*To add to the fun on Christmas morning, I always top this casserole
with a fresh parsley and red bell pepper "wreath!"*

3 c. Cheddar cheese, shredded
3 c. mozzarella cheese, shredded
1/4 c. mushrooms, sliced
1/4 c. green onions, sliced
1/4 c. margarine

8 oz. cooked ham, diced
1/2 c. all-purpose flour
1-3/4 c. milk
1 T. fresh parsley, chopped
8 eggs, beaten

In a large bowl, lightly toss cheeses together. Sprinkle half of cheese
mixture in an ungreased 13"x9" baking dish. In medium skillet, cook
mushrooms and onions in margarine. Arrange vegetables over cheese,
layer ham on vegetables. Sprinkle remaining cheese over ham. In
large bowl, using a wire whisk, blend flour, milk, parsley and eggs;
pour over casserole. Bake at 350 degrees for 35 to 45 minutes or until
mixture is set and top is lightly browned. Let stand 10 minutes.
Makes 10 servings.

*Fill a large pickle jar
with a pillar candle, then
surround it with an
assortment of colorful
buttons. A whimsical gift
for a crafty friend!*

Frosty Mornings

Christmas Morn' Casserole ✓

Sally Burke
Lansing, MI

Always a favorite!

12 bread slices, crusts trimmed
    and one side buttered
5-oz. jar bacon bits
8-oz. pkg. Cheddar cheese,
    grated and divided

1 tomato, thinly sliced
6 eggs
3 c. milk
1 t. dry mustard

Coat a 13"x9" glass baking dish with non-stick spray. Place 6 slices of bread, buttered side up, in baking dish, fitting slices to shape of pan. Sprinkle on bacon bits and half of the cheese. Top with remaining bread slices, buttered side up. Place one or 2 tomato slices on top of each bread slice. Beat together eggs, milk and mustard. Pour over casserole; refrigerate, covered, overnight. Bake, uncovered, at 350 degrees for one hour. Cut into squares and serve.

The only things we ever keep are what we give away.

-Louis Ginsberg

Dublin Potato Pancake

Virginia Konerman
Virginia Beach, VA

Yummy with eggs and bacon...a hearty farmhouse breakfast!

2 potatoes, grated
1 egg, beaten
1 onion, finely chopped
1/2 c. Cheddar cheese, shredded

2 bacon slices, cooked and
  chopped
salt and pepper to taste

Mix all ingredients together in a bowl. Spray a skillet with non-stick spray and place over medium-high heat until warm. Pour potato mixture into skillet, pressing down to form a pancake. Cook over medium-high heat until golden brown on the bottom and middle is set. Check edges periodically by gently lifting. Turn pancake using 2 spatulas and cook second side until golden.

Tiny potted trees can be tucked into a variety of fun containers...baskets, old wooden cranberry boxes, painted pails or all wrapped up in cozy flannel-covered buckets.

Welcome Friends

Baked Pralines & Brie

Mandy Mackey
Dumfries, VA

Great for holiday parties!

1/3 c. pecan pieces
8-oz. brie round

1/3 c. brown sugar, packed
1/4 to 1/2 c. honey

Toast pecans by spreading them on a cookie sheet and baking at 375 degrees for 5 minutes. Shake the cookie sheet often and watch carefully. Set aside to cool. Place brie in a small oven-safe baking dish. Sprinkle with brown sugar and pecans. Drizzle enough honey over brie to cover toppings. Bake at 400 degrees until topping is bubbly. Remove and serve immediately with crackers.

Holiday Cheese Ball

Mary Kay Drayton
Fenton, MI

This tasty recipe is one we always enjoy on Christmas day!

1 t. onion juice
1 t. Worcestershire sauce
1/2 c. fresh parsley, chopped
8-oz. pkg. cream cheese
1/2-lb. sharp Cheddar cheese,
    grated

4-oz. blue cheese wedge
3/4 c. chopped pecans, divided
Garnish: pecans and fresh
    parsley

Combine first 6 ingredients together in a mixing bowl, stir in 1/2 cup pecans and shape into a ball. Roll cheese ball in 1/4 cup of pecans. Garnish with whole pecans and fresh parsley. Let stand at room temperature for one hour before serving.

Welcome Friends

Lemon & Dijon Chicken Wings

Penny Stuart
North Pole, AK

My family loves this recipe...they say it's because of my secret sauce!

2 lbs. frozen chicken wings
1 T. Worcestershire sauce
1 T. lemon juice
1 T. lime juice

2 T. Dijon mustard
1 t. garlic, minced
1/2 c. margarine

Bake frozen chicken wings in an oiled 13"x9" glass casserole dish at 450 degrees for 1-1/2 hours, just until browned; drain fat. Mix the remaining ingredients together and microwave on medium for 2 minutes or until margarine is melted. Pour sauce mixture over chicken and stir to coat. Return chicken to oven for 30 minutes more or until crispy.

Garlic-Feta Cheese Spread

Elizabeth McKay
Romeoville, IL

This is a real winner!

1 garlic clove, minced
1/4 t. salt
1/2 lb. Feta cheese, crumbled
1/2 c. mayonnaise
1/4 t. dried marjoram

1/4 t. dried dill weed, crumbled
1/4 t. dried basil, crumbled
1/4 t. dried thyme, crumbled
3/4 lb. cream cheese, softened

Using a fork, mash garlic into a paste; add salt. Using a food processor, blend together Feta cheese, mayonnaise, garlic mixture, herbs and cream cheese. Spoon into a crock and chill, covered, for 2 hours. Makes 1-1/2 cups. Serve with crackers, bagel chips or slices of pita bread.

Make a snowflake garland for your tree. Use lengths of butcher paper, fold and cut as you would for a paper doll chain. Unfold and wrap around your tree.

Pam's Spinach Squares

Pam Hilton
Centerburg, OH

A tasty appetizer you can make ahead of time.

1 c. all-purpose flour
1 t. salt
1 t. baking powder
2 eggs, beaten
1 c. milk
1 stick butter, melted

10-oz. pkg. frozen, chopped
   spinach, thawed and drained
1 lb. sharp Cheddar cheese,
   grated
1 onion, chopped

Combine flour, salt and baking powder. Add eggs, milk and butter; stir. Add remaining ingredients and pour into a lightly oiled 13"x9" pan. Bake at 350 degrees for 35 minutes or until bubbly around edges. Cut into 50 squares and serve warm. If preparing ahead of time, let cool, then cut into squares. Place on cookie sheets in freezer until frozen, remove from cookie sheets and place squares in freezer bags and return to freezer. To serve, heat squares for 20 minutes at 350 degrees or until lightly browned at edges.

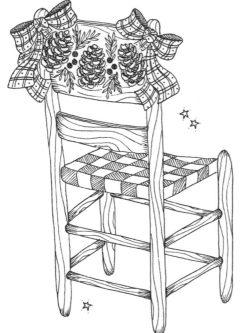

Miniature swags look festive tied to the backs of chairs. Just fashion swags from fresh greenery, pine cones and ribbon. Add an extra length of ribbon for hanging, then slip over the chair backs.

Welcome Friends

Beef & Sausage Spread

Cheryl Volbruck
Costa Mesa, CA

This recipe is a "must" whenever we're expecting guests. I can start it in the morning and it's ready when my guests arrive. They'll ask you for your recipe, I promise!

3/4 c. onions, sautéed
1 T. butter
2 lbs. ground beef, browned

1 lb. ground sausage, browned
2 lbs. pasteurized processed
   cheese spread, diced

Sauté onions in butter, combine with beef and sausage in slow cooker. Cover and cook on low for 4 to 6 hours. Drain off fat and add cheese. Stir cheese until melted and blended with the meat and onion mixture. Keep warm and serve on small rye rounds or your favorite crackers.

Crabmeat Pastry Shells

Linda Scott-Hoag
Janesville, WI

Looks elegant and tastes great!

6-oz. can crabmeat
2 oz. cream cheese, softened
1/4 to 1/2 c. mayonnaise
3 T. green onion, chopped

1 t. Worcestershire sauce
1 t. lemon juice
10-oz. pkg. pastry shells

Mix first 6 ingredients together and refrigerate overnight. Fill pastry shells. Keep refrigerated until ready to serve.

Wire together several jingle bells, then top with a homespun bow and a loop. Slipped over a doorknob, they'll joyfully greet all your holiday guests!

Onion Blossom

Hope Boudreaux
Franklin, LA

Serve with a variety of dipping sauces…blue cheese, ranch or cajun.

4 onions
2-1/2 c. all-purpose flour,
   divided
4 t. paprika
2 t. garlic powder

1/2 t. pepper
1/4 t. cayenne pepper
1/2 c. cornstarch
1 c. water
oil

Cut off the top portion of each onion and peel away first layer of onion skin. Make several vertical slices through onions, being careful not to cut through the bottom of the onion. Allow onions to sit in ice water, covered, for about 4 hours to open. Combine 2 cups flour and spices. Dip onions in seasoned flour mixture; shake off excess. In separate bowl, combine remaining flour, cornstarch and water. Dip onion in second batter; shake off excess mixture. In a deep fryer add enough oil to cover onion and fry each onion at about 350 degrees for approximately 5 to 7 minutes.

Bring the outdoors inside for the holidays!
Top your mantel with tiny hemlocks tucked in
terra cotta pots, birdhouses, blooming paperwhites
or amaryllis and pine cones piled under a bell jar.

Welcome Friends

Warm Artichoke Dip

Irene Robinson
Cincinnati, OH

I'm always asked to share the recipe for this wonderful appetizer.

10-oz. pkg. frozen, chopped
   spinach, thawed and drained
14-oz. can artichoke hearts,
   drained and chopped
1-1/2 c. Monterey Jack cheese,
   grated

3/4 c. half-and-half
1/2 t. pepper
3/4 t. salt
1 garlic clove, pressed

Stir together all ingredients and pour into a one-quart casserole dish.
Bake, uncovered, at 350 degrees for 20 to 25 minutes.

Creamy Blue Cheese Ball

Liz Koeplin
Dublin, OH

A military wife shared this recipe with me 25 years ago.
I hope you'll enjoy it as much as I have.

3/4 to 1 c. walnuts, toasted
8-oz. pkg. cream cheese,
   softened
3 to 4 oz. crumbled blue cheese

1 T. green pepper, finely chopped
1 T. pimento, finely chopped
garlic salt to taste

Toast walnuts by spreading them on a cookie sheet and baking
them at 375 degrees for 5 minutes. Shake the sheet often and
watch carefully. Set aside to cool. Blend together all ingredients
except walnuts and shape into a ball. Chill one hour then roll in nuts.

Winter is the time for comfort, for good food and
warmth, for the touch of a friendly hand and for a
talk beside the fire; it is the time for home.

–Edith Sitwell

Bite-Size Cheese Balls

Carol Hickman
Kingsport, TN

Instead of having one large cheese ball, consider making these!

2 3-oz. pkgs. cream cheese,
    softened
2 c. Cheddar cheese, finely
    shredded

1-1/2 c. carrots, finely shredded
2 t. honey
1 c. pecans, finely chopped
4 doz. pretzel sticks

Combine cheeses, carrots and honey; chill for one hour. Shape into one-inch balls and then roll in pecans. Chill, then insert pretzel sticks before serving. Makes about 45 cheese balls.

Artichoke Salsa

Rhonda Craig
Greenwell Springs, LA

Serve with crispy chips or crackers.

6-oz. jar marinated artichoke
    hearts, chopped, liquid
    reserved
1 tomato, chopped

1 red onion, diced
1/4 t. salt
1 t. lime juice

In medium bowl, place artichoke hearts, reserved liquid, tomato, onion, salt and lime juice. Stir until well blended. Serve immediately or chill and serve.

*At Christmas, play
and make good cheer,
for Christmas comes
but once a year!*

-Thomas Tusser

Welcome Friends

Black Bean Dip

Barb Traxler
Mankato, MN

This terrific dip always seems to be a big hit!

15-oz. can black beans, rinsed
   and drained
4-1/4 oz. can black olives,
   chopped
1 onion, finely chopped
1 to 2 garlic cloves, finely
   minced
2 T. olive oil
2 T. lime juice

1/4 t. salt
1/4 t. crushed red pepper
1/4 t. cumin
1/8 t. pepper
8-oz. pkg. cream cheese,
   softened
2 eggs, hard-boiled and sliced
2 green onions, sliced
1 tomato, finely chopped

Mix beans, olives, onion, garlic, olive oil, lime juice, salt, red pepper, cumin and pepper together. Cover and refrigerate at least 2 hours. Spread cream cheese on bottom of serving plate. Spoon bean mixture evenly over cream cheese. Arrange eggs on top of bean mixture in a ring around edge of plate. Sprinkle top with green onions and tomato. Serve with tortilla chips.

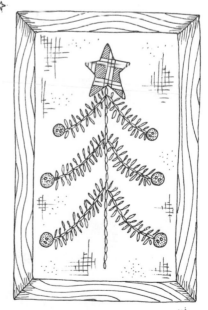

Turn a sideboard into a winter wonderland! Cover it with a white fleece blanket then add reminders of winter fun...a pair of ice skates or snowshoes, a miniature sled and lots of pictures of the family building snowmen, skiing or bringing home the tree!

Chicken Enchilada Dip

Diane Sybert
Athens, IL

Serve this spicy dip with tortilla chips...yummy!

3 chicken breast halves
8-oz. pkg. cream cheese,
　softened
1-1/3 c. Cheddar cheese, grated
1 t. garlic, minced
1-1/2 T. chili powder
1 t. cumin
1 t. dry oregano

1 t. paprika
cayenne pepper to taste
hot pepper sauce to taste
1 bunch cilantro leaves, chopped
4 green onions, chopped
10-oz. can diced tomatoes with
　green chilies

Place chicken in enough water to cover; cook over low heat for
30 minutes or until juices run clear; set aside to cool. When chicken
is cool enough to handle, remove skin and bone; discard. Finely chop
chicken; set aside. In a large mixing bowl, mix cheeses until creamy
and well blended. Add garlic, chili powder, cumin, oregano, paprika,
cayenne pepper and pepper sauce; mix well. Add chicken, cilantro,
green onions and tomatoes. Gently fold into the cheese mixture.
Refrigerate overnight for full flavor. Makes about 6 cups.

*Fill a ladle with a
scoop of your
favorite potpourri
and a votive.
It looks so
old-fashioned
hanging on your
kitchen wall!*

Welcome Friends

Mini Ham Puffs

Kristine Marumoto
Salt Lake City, UT

Serve these warm from the oven with Dijon mustard.

1/4 lb. cooked ham, finely
    chopped
1 onion, finely chopped
1/2 c. Swiss cheese, shredded
1 egg, beaten

1-1/2 t. Dijon mustard
1/8 t. pepper
8-oz. tube refrigerated crescent
    rolls

Place ham and onion in mixing bowl. Add cheese, egg, mustard and pepper; mix well. Lightly spray muffin pan with non-stick spray. Unroll crescent rolls and press dough into large rectangle. Cut rectangle into 24 pieces using pizza cutter. Press dough pieces into muffin cups. Fill each muffin cup with ham filling. Bake at 350 degrees for 13 to 15 minutes or until lightly browned. Makes approximately 24 appetizers.

Parmesan-Spinach Balls

Donna Fields
Martinsburg, WV

You can also spoon this into a one-quart casserole, bake and serve as a wonderful, warm spinach dip.

2 10-oz. pkgs. frozen, chopped
    spinach, cooked and drained
6 eggs, beaten
2 onions, chopped

1-1/2 sticks butter, melted
1/2 c. grated Parmesan cheese
2 c. stuffing mix

Mix all ingredients together. To serve several guests, use an ice cream scoop to shape mixture into large balls, or for individual servings, make smaller walnut-size balls. Place on a lightly oiled baking sheet and bake at 350 degrees for 20 minutes. Serve with crackers.

Brown Sugar Meatballs ✓

Brenda Derby
Northborough, MA

*Everyone will love these meatballs; the brown sugar and
soy sauce give them a tangy taste!*

1-1/2 lbs. ground beef
1 onion, minced
3/4 c. quick-cooking oatmeal
1/2 c. milk
1 egg, beaten
1 t. salt
1/2 t. pepper

2 T. oil
1 c. beef broth
1/4 c. vinegar
3/4 c. catsup
2 T. brown sugar, packed
1/8 c. soy sauce

Mix ground beef with onion, oatmeal, milk, egg, salt and pepper.
Form into balls, place in skillet and brown in hot oil. To the same
skillet, add beef broth; cover and simmer for one hour. In a small
saucepan, combine vinegar, catsup, brown sugar and soy sauce
over medium-high heat. When mixture is hot, pour over meatballs.

*Not believe in Santa Claus?
You might as well not believe in fairies.*

-Frances P. Church

Welcome Friends

Herb-Marinated Cheese

*Lynne Tharan
New Bethlehem, PA*

Yummy with sourdough bread.

4 to 6 oz. sharp Cheddar cheese, cubed
4 to 6 oz. Provolone cheese, cubed
1/2 c. olive oil
1/2 t. peppercorns
1 bay leaf
1/4 c. herbal vinegar
1/4 t. fennel seed
1 T. fresh parsley, chopped
3 to 4 garlic cloves, pressed

Combine all ingredients in bowl with tight fitting lid; refrigerate and marinate for one to 4 days, stirring and mixing each day. Remove cheese from bowl with slotted spoon and serve with toothpicks.

Crescent Chicken Bites

*Kelley Hahn
Heath, OH*

Very good and so easy!

8-oz. tube refrigerated crescent rolls
3-oz. pkg. cream cheese, softened
4 T. margarine, melted and divided
2 c. chicken, cooked and cubed
1/4 t. salt
1/8 t. pepper
2 T. onion, chopped
2 c. seasoned croutons, crushed

Separate crescent rolls into 4 rectangles; seal perforations and set aside. Blend cream cheese and 2 tablespoons margarine until smooth. Add next 4 ingredients; mix well. Spoon 1/2 cup of chicken mixture into the center of each rectangle; pull corners of dough to center of mixture and seal. Brush tops with remaining margarine. Sprinkle with croutons. Bake on an ungreased cookie sheet for 20 to 25 minutes at 350 degrees or until golden brown. Slice in half to serve. Makes 8 servings.

BLT Squares

Janet Welch
Pontiac, IL

I made this for a party when the hostess requested I bring "something cold." It was an instant hit!

10-oz. tube pizza crust
8-oz. pkg. cream cheese
1 c. mayonnaise-type salad
    dressing

1/2 lettuce head, finely shredded
1 tomato, diced
3-oz. jar bacon bits

Spray a 13"x9" pan with non-stick spray, unroll and press pizza crust to fit pan. Prick with fork, then bake at 425 degrees for about 8 to 9 minutes or until golden; cool. Mix cream cheese and mayonnaise-type salad dressing until smooth. Spread over cooled crust. Top with lettuce, tomato and bacon. Cut into squares. Do not prepare more than 2 to 3 hours in advance.

Create a festive placecard! Using decorative-edge scissors, cut out a 2"x1" square from heavy card stock and write a guest's name on it. Punch a hole near one corner, slip a length of ribbon through the hole and tie to a star-shaped cookie cutter!

Welcome Friends

Pepperoni Puffs

Marcia Marcoux
Charlton, MA

Tasty bite-size puffs!

1 c. all-purpose flour
1 c. milk
1 c. Cheddar cheese, grated

1 t. baking powder
1 egg
1-1/2 c. pepperoni, diced

Combine first 5 ingredients until well mixed. Add pepperoni and allow to stand for 15 minutes. Grease mini muffin pan and fill 3/4 full. Bake at 350 degrees for 25 to 35 minutes or until golden brown.

Seafood Fondue

Kim Brown
Goodrich, MI

Our whole family loves this!

10-3/4 oz. can cream of shrimp
  soup
1/2 c. milk
1-1/2 c. Cheddar cheese,
  shredded

1/4 c. Swiss cheese, shredded
6-oz. can crabmeat
1 French bread loaf, cut in
  bite-size pieces

Blend together first 5 ingredients in a double boiler until cheeses melt. Transfer mixture to a fondue pot or serve in a slow cooker on low heat. Dip pieces of French bread into fondue.

If you know someone who's a music lover,
cover their gift boxes with sheet music!
Look for single pages of nostalgic sheet music
at flea markets or tag sales.

Pineapple Welcome Dip

Gentry Barrett
Holly Springs, NC

This is truly a "welcome" dip...it's perfect for guests to enjoy when they first arrive!

2 8-oz. pkgs. cream cheese, softened
1 c. mayonnaise

15-1/4 oz. can crushed pineapple, drained

Mix together cream cheese, mayonnaise and pineapple. Stir and chill thoroughly. Serve with a variety of crackers.

Lemony Fruit Dip

Sheldon Marumoto
Salt Lake City, UT

Tasty served with fresh fruit slices!

2 eggs
1 c. sugar, divided
1/3 c. lemon juice
1 T. cornstarch

1/2 c. water
1 t. vanilla extract
1 c. whipping cream, whipped

In small bowl, beat eggs, 1/2 cup sugar and lemon juice until frothy; set aside. In medium saucepan, combine remaining 1/2 cup sugar and cornstarch. Gradually add water; mixing well. Over medium heat, cook and stir until thickened and clear; remove from heat. Gradually beat in egg mixture. Return to low heat, cook and stir until slightly thickened. Remove from heat and stir in vanilla. Cool, then fold in whipped cream and chill.

Christmas! The very word brings joy to our hearts!

–Joan Winmill Brown

Welcome Friends

Sugar & Spice Walnuts

Debra Severdia
Santa Rosa, CA

*Tasty to snack on, they also make great gifts. Just pack into a
pretty jar, tin or crock and tie on a raffia bow!*

1 c. sugar	6 T. milk
1/4 t. salt	2-1/2 c. walnuts
1/2 to 1 t. cinnamon	1 t. vanilla extract

Combine sugar, salt, cinnamon and milk in large saucepan. Cook over
medium-high heat, stirring constantly until the mixture reaches the
soft ball stage, about 234 to 240 degrees on a candy thermometer.
Remove from heat, add walnuts and vanilla. Mix well until nuts are
coated and spread in a single layer on a sheet of wax paper to cool.

*Host a holiday tea party for your friends.
It's so nice to relax and catch up
with one another.*

Sweet & Sour Vegetable Dip

Lori Graham
Lancaster, PA

*Spoon into a bowl and surround with crispy crackers
and pretzels or lots of crunchy vegetables.*

2 T. sugar
2 T. vinegar
2 eggs
8-oz. pkg. cream cheese,
    softened

1 onion, finely chopped
1 green pepper, finely chopped
1/2 c. bacon, crisply cooked and
    crumbled

Mix sugar and vinegar together in a saucepan over medium heat.
Add eggs and beat until well blended. Cook until mixture thickens,
stirring constantly. Add cream cheese; stir well. Remove from heat,
add onion, green pepper and bacon; stir. Chill before serving.

Sprinkle snow-covered stars everywhere! Draw a star pattern on scrap wood, cut with a jig saw, then paint stars with white latex paint. You can even mix a little sawdust in the paint for texture. Let dry, drill a small hole at the top of each star, insert a length of wire and hang them on your tree, mantel or garland.

Welcome Friends

Applesauce Meatballs

June Cavarretta
West Dundee, IL

This recipe was shared by a neighbor, Mrs. Burke. She was so appreciative when my husband shoveled her drive on a snowy winter day she baked these for him...I could hardly resist eating them all!

1 egg
1-1/2 lbs. ground beef
2 c. corn flake cereal, slightly
   crushed
3 T. onion, chopped
1/4 t. sage

1/8 t. pepper
1-1/2 t. salt
1/8 t. baking powder
2/3 c. applesauce
10-3/4 oz. can tomato soup
1/2 c. water

Beat egg; add remaining ingredients except soup and water. Shape meat into walnut-size balls and place in a shallow baking dish. Mix soup and water, pour over meatballs. Bake at 350 degrees for one hour, basting occasionally

Hot Crab Canapés

DeNeane Deskins
Marengo, OH

One of Mom's favorites; every time I make it, I think of home.

1/2 lb. crabmeat, shredded
8-oz. pkg. sharp Cheddar
   cheese, shredded
2 eggs, hard-boiled and finely
   chopped
1/4 c. mayonnaise

salt and pepper to taste
1/8 t. garlic powder
2 T. onion, grated
1 T. fresh parsley, minced
20 bread slices

Combine first 8 ingredients; set aside. Cut each bread slice into 4 squares. Spread each square with crab mixture and place on an ungreased baking sheet. Bake at 350 degrees for 10 to 15 minutes or until lightly browned. Makes 6 dozen.

Crab-Stuffed Mushrooms

Nicole Shira
New Baltimore, MI

A delicious appetizer...plan to make extras!

6-oz. can crabmeat
1/2 c. butter, melted
1/3 c. bread crumbs
3/4 c. grated Parmesan cheese
2 to 3 garlic cloves, chopped

1/4 to 1/2 c. onion, chopped
salt and pepper to taste
12-oz. pkg. fresh mushrooms,
   caps washed and stems
   removed

Mix all ingredients together, except mushrooms. Stuff mushroom caps with crab mixture and place on a lightly oiled baking sheet. Bake at 375 degrees for 20 minutes.

California Zippy Dip

Linda Shupe
Baltimore, MD

This dip is wonderful for all your favorite vegetables...mushrooms,
zucchini, carrots and peppers!

1/2 t. cinnamon
1/2 t. ginger
1/2 t. curry powder
1/2 t. cayenne pepper
1/2 t. salt

1/2 t. onion salt
1/2 t. garlic salt
1 pt. sour cream
1 pt. mayonnaise

Blend all ingredients well. Refrigerate at least one hour before serving.

For an easy-to-make primitive ornament,
hot glue a rusty tin star or snowflake to the
front of a tea-stained mitten!

Welcome Friends

Parmesan Chicken Wings

Jan Sofranko
Malta, IL

Everyone's favorite and just perfect for a holiday buffet!

1/2 c. margarine	1 t. salt
2 T. dried parsley	1/2 t. pepper
1 T. dried oregano	1 c. grated Parmesan cheese
2 t. paprika	4 lbs. chicken wings

Melt margarine in a small bowl. Mix dry ingredients and cheese in another small bowl. Dip the wings in the margarine and then in the dry ingredients. Arrange on a foil-lined baking sheet coated with non-stick spray. Drizzle wings with any margarine remaining in your bowl and bake at 350 degrees for about one hour.

Dress up your door with a garland of fresh evergreens.
Just wire bunches of greenery on a length of roping
that's long enough to circle your door then tie on
tin stars, raffia bows, pine cones or fresh fruit.

Mushroom-Broccoli Dip

Heather Porter
Villa Park, IL

You can add a bit more horseradish if you like a stronger flavor.

1 onion, chopped
3 celery stalks, chopped
1 stick butter
garlic salt and pepper to taste
2 T. all-purpose flour
1/4 t. creamy horseradish
10-3/4 oz. can cream of
   mushroom soup

4-oz. can mushroom pieces
8-oz. pkg. sharp Cheddar
   cheese, shredded
8-oz. can chicken
2 10-oz. pkgs. frozen broccoli,
   cooked and drained
salt and pepper to taste

Sauté onion and celery in butter, add garlic salt and pepper. Stir in flour to make a roux. Cook for 3 to 4 minutes, stirring constantly. Add horseradish, soup and mushrooms. Stir until bubbly. Add cheese and chicken; stir until cheese melts, remove from heat and add broccoli. Salt and pepper to taste, then transfer to a chafing dish to keep warm.

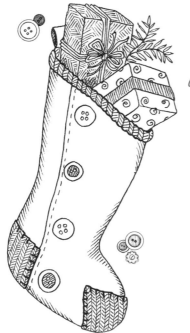

A gift any new mom will really love! Search flea markets or book shops for old-fashioned nursery rhyme books in less-than-perfect condition. They're filled with charming pictures that would be darling framed in a baby's room!

Welcome Friends

Cherry Tomato Appetizers

Donna Messer
Cincinnati, OH

Make these early the day of your open house, just refrigerate until guests arrive!

1 pt. cherry tomatoes
salt to taste
8 bacon slices, crisply cooked
   and crumbled

1/2 c. mayonnaise
1 shallot, finely chopped
Garnish: fresh parsley

Cut a thin slice off the round end of each tomato; tomatoes will sit on the stem end. Using a small sharp knife or a melon ball scoop, remove the seeds and juice from the center of each tomato, leaving the shell. Salt the inside of tomato shells and drain upside down on a paper towel for at least 1/2 hour or overnight in the refrigerator. Mix bacon, mayonnaise and shallot. Take a small spoon and stuff each tomato with mixture, garnish with parsley. Makes 24 appetizers.

Tasty Feta Spread

Nan Wright
Houston, TX

Spoon into a crock and serve with bagel or pita chips.

1/2 lb. feta cheese, crumbled
8-oz. pkg. cream cheese

6 to 8 oz. refrigerated pesto

Blend together feta and cream cheese in a food processor. Add prepared pesto, found in the refrigerator section of your grocery store, and process until smooth. Refrigerate 4 hours so flavors can blend.

Fill baskets with apples, popcorn and peanuts...great for munching on while enjoying a holiday movie!

Creamy Vanilla Fruit Dip

Patti Johnson
Radcliff, KY

This couldn't be easier to prepare! Spoon into a hollowed-out melon and serve with lots of fresh fruit...strawberries, apples, cantaloupe, grapes and honeydew are all great!

1-1/2 c. cold buttermilk
3-oz. pkg. instant vanilla
    pudding mix

8 oz. whipped topping

Combine buttermilk and pudding with electric mixer for 2 minutes. Fold in whipped topping. Chill for at least 2 hours.

Help the kids make a fun wintertime snowman ornament; it's so easy! Add a few drops of white acrylic paint inside a clear, glass ball. Swirl the paint around to thoroughly coat the inside; remove any excess. When the paint has dried, add eyes, a nose and mouth to the outside using black and orange acrylic paint.

Hearty Holiday Fare

Mom's Turkey Pot Pie
2 c. turkey

Prosciutto & Mushroom Chicken *Jo Ann*

Our kids really love this. I always have to double the recipe.

4 boneless, skinless chicken
   breasts
1/2 t. garlic, minced
1/4 lb. prosciutto, diced
1/2 lb. mushrooms, sliced

2 T. olive oil, divided
2 T. butter
2 t. fresh parsley, minced
1 T. lemon juice
1/4 t. pepper

Wrap each chicken breast between two sheets of wax paper. Use a
meat mallet to gently pound chicken until it's 1/4-inch thick. Place
chicken in refrigerator until ready to cook. Sauté garlic, prosciutto and
mushrooms in one tablespoon of olive oil for 15 to 20 minutes. Spoon
sautéed mixture into a bowl and set aside. In the same skillet, heat
remaining oil and butter together. Place chicken in a single layer in
skillet. Cook, turning once, until cooked through; about 5 minutes,
or until juices run clear when chicken is pierced. Return mushroom
mixture to skillet and stir in parsley, lemon juice and pepper. Cook,
covered, until thoroughly heated about 2 to 3 minutes. When ready
to serve place chicken on plates and top with mushroom sauce.
Makes 4 servings.

*Set a cinnamon pillar candle in a small tin
pail, then surround it with rosehips.*

Hearty Holiday Fare

Fruited Pork Loin

Tina Wright
Atlanta, GA

Slices of this pork loin make a beautiful holiday presentation.

1/2 c. pitted dates, coarsely
   chopped
1/4 c. dried apricots, coarsely
   chopped
1/4 c. pecans, finely chopped
1 garlic clove, minced
1-1/2 t. dried thyme, crushed

2 T. molasses, divided
1/2 t. salt, divided
1/4 t. pepper
2-lb. boneless pork loin roast
2/3 c. bourbon
2/3 c. chicken broth
1/4 c. light cream

Blend together dates, apricots, pecans, garlic, thyme, one tablespoon molasses, 1/4 teaspoon salt and pepper; set aside. To cut pork roast in a double-butterfly; begin at one end of the roast and cut horizontally almost all the way through; lay roast flat, like an open book. Starting at the center of the open loin, cut horizontally again on the left portion; begin at the center again and repeat with the right portion. You should now have a long, flat roast. Spread date mixture evenly over open roast and starting with the short end, roll up stuffed roast jelly roll-style. Tie roast securely every 2 to 3 inches with kitchen string and lay roast in a shallow, roasting pan; set aside. Blend together bourbon, chicken broth and remaining molasses in a small saucepan. Bring mixture to a boil and pour over roast. Roast pork at 350 degrees for one hour, basting occasionally. Remove roast from roasting pan, reserve drippings and set aside. Stir together cream and 1/4 teaspoon salt in a small saucepan; blend in reserved drippings. Cook over medium heat, stirring constantly, until mixture thickens. Slice roast and serve with cream sauce.

When Christmas day comes
there is still the same warm feeling
we had as children, the same warmth
that enfolds our hearts and our homes.

–Joan Winmill Brown

Turkey & Rice Casserole

Yvonne Torland
Burnsville, MN

*I've made this recipe many times and often substitute
chicken for turkey...it's just as tasty!*

1 c. celery, chopped
1 T. butter
2 c. turkey, cooked and chopped
1 c. rice, cooked
8-oz. can water chestnuts,
   drained and sliced
3 eggs, hard-boiled and chopped
3/4 c. mayonnaise
1 t. onion, minced

1 t. lemon juice
1 t. salt
14-1/2 oz. can cream of
   mushroom soup
1 c. potato chips, crushed
1 T. slivered almonds
1/4 c. butter, melted
2-oz. jar pimentos

Sauté celery in butter until tender. In a large bowl, mix turkey, celery,
rice, water chestnuts and eggs together. In a separate bowl, blend
together mayonnaise, onion, lemon juice, salt and soup. Fold
mayonnaise mixture into turkey mixture. Spoon into a lightly oiled
2-quart casserole dish. Top with potato chips and almonds; drizzle
with butter and sprinkle with pimentos. Bake at 350 degrees for 35 to
40 minutes. Makes 10 to 12 servings.

*Tuck some plump, handmade, homespun hearts into a
yellowware bowl and set by your door. Guests will
love taking one home as a reminder of their visit!*

Hearty Holiday Fare

Chicken Quiche

Wendy Paffenroth
Pine Island, NY

This recipe is easily doubled; just use 2 pie crusts pressed into a 13"x9" pan and bake about 15 minutes longer. It's great when you're expecting extra holiday guests!

9-inch pie crust
4 oz. Monterey Jack cheese, shredded
1/4 c. mozzarella cheese, shredded
2 T. all-purpose flour
1 T. chicken bouillon
2 c. chicken, cooked and diced

1 c. milk
3 eggs, beaten
1/4 c. onion, diced
1/8 t. pepper
1/8 t. dried chives
1/8 t. dried parsley
1/2 t. paprika

Bake pie crust at 425 degrees for approximately 8 minutes. Remove from oven and turn heat down to 350 degrees. In a medium bowl, mix the cheeses with the flour and bouillon. Mix in the remaining ingredients and stir well. Pour into pie crust and sprinkle top with paprika. Bake about 40 to 45 minutes or until set. Remove from oven and let set for 10 minutes before serving. Makes 6 servings.

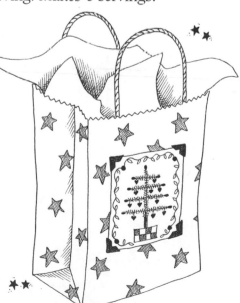

Stitch a simple feather tree design on a square of unbleached muslin. Then look through grandma's button box to find small buttons and charms to stitch on the tree as ornaments...so pretty!

Ginger-Pepper Steak

Mary Bird
Jacksonville, FL

Serve over white rice...a tasty way to end a day of holiday shopping!

1/4 c. soy sauce	2 T. oil
1 c. beef bouillon	3 green peppers, cut into strips
2 garlic cloves, pressed	1 onion, cut into strips
1/2 t. ginger	3 T. cornstarch
2-lb. round steak, cut into strips	1/4 c. water

Mix soy sauce, bouillon, garlic and ginger. Marinate meat in mixture for at least 2 hours. Reserve 1/2 cup of marinade, drain the meat and set aside. Heat oil in wok or very large frying pan, stir-fry the meat, green pepper and onion 3 to 5 minutes; add the marinade. Blend together cornstarch and water; add to wok. Simmer until thick.

A painted pail or sap bucket is perfect for holding everything you'll need to start a cozy fire on a chilly winter night! Lots of pine cones, fatwood sticks, fireplace matches, sprigs of dried herbs and twigs can be tucked inside.

Lemon-Broiled Salmon

Tori Willis
Champaign, IL

This cooks quickly making it perfect for a holiday brunch.

4 salmon steaks
1 stick butter, melted
salt and pepper to taste

2 t. fresh dill weed, chopped
2 t. fresh parsley, chopped
juice of one lemon

Brush each salmon steak with one tablespoon butter; set aside. Blend remaining butter with salt, pepper, dill weed, parsley and lemon juice. Place salmon under broiler and broil 5 minutes; turn. Brush on butter mixture then broil the second side for 5 minutes. Makes 4 servings.

Christmas is not a time nor a season,
but a state of mind. To cherish peace and
goodwill...is to have the real spirit of Christmas.

-Calvin Coolidge

Roasted Vegetables & Pasta

Gail Prather
Bethel, MN

Roasting vegetables in your oven is so easy and your kitchen will be filled with a wonderful aroma!

2 T. olive oil
1 t. fresh thyme, chopped
2 t. garlic, finely chopped
1/2 t. salt
1-1/2 c. asparagus, chopped
1-1/2 c. baby carrots, quartered
1-1/2 c. red pepper, sliced
1 c. leeks, sliced

1 c. rutabaga, cubed
8 oz. angel hair pasta, uncooked
1/4 c. fresh parsley, chopped
2 T. butter, melted
1 t. lemon zest
Garnish: grated Parmesan
   cheese

In a small bowl, stir together oil, thyme, garlic and salt. Place vegetables in 13"x9" baking pan. Spoon oil mixture over vegetables; toss well to coat. Cover pan with aluminum foil. Bake, stirring occasionally, at 400 degrees for about 25 minutes. Uncover; continue baking for 15 to 20 minutes, stirring once, or until vegetables are tender and starting to brown. Meanwhile, cook pasta according to package directions; drain. Toss hot pasta with parsley, butter and lemon zest. Spoon vegetables over pasta mixture. Sprinkle with cheese. Makes 4 servings.

Old architectural stars look great lined along a mantel or window sill, scattered along the center of a buffet table or sitting under a pillar candle.

Hearty Holiday Fare

Ginger Chicken

Susie Knupp
Bailey, CO

Add a pinch more ginger and garlic if you'd like this a little tangier.

4 boneless, skinless chicken
    breasts
1/3 c. all-purpose flour
1 T. oil
1/2 c. pineapple juice

2 T. honey
2 T. soy sauce
1/2 t. ginger
2 t. garlic, minced

Coat chicken pieces with flour. Heat oil in a non-stick skillet over medium-high heat. Cook chicken 3 to 4 minutes per side until lightly browned on the outside. Meanwhile, mix pineapple juice, honey, soy sauce, ginger and garlic; pour over the chicken. Cook, stirring constantly, until juices run clear when chicken is pierced and the sauce is slightly thickened. If sauce is too thick, add 1/4 cup of water. Makes 4 servings.

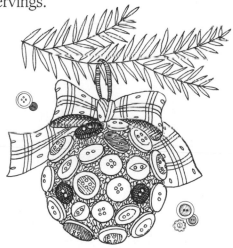

Make an easy, old-fashioned looking ornament. Coat a foam ball with a light layer of acrylic paint, red or green would be perfect. Use a hot glue gun to attach several different colors and styles of buttons, then just add a loop for hanging.

Best-Ever Meatloaf

Terri Lewis
Fairview Park, OH

I've had this recipe for many years and my husband loves it.
He always told me he didn't like meatloaf, but you'd never
believe it by the way he enjoys this...it's delicious!

2 t. butter
3/4 c. onion, chopped
3/4 c. scallions, sliced
1/2 c. red pepper, chopped
2 t. garlic, minced
2 eggs
3/4 c. catsup, divided
1/2 c. milk
1 T. plus 1 t. Worcestershire
  sauce
1/2 t. salt
2 lbs. ground beef
12 oz. ground sausage
3/4 c. bread crumbs

Melt butter in large non-stick skillet. Add onion, scallions, pepper and garlic. Cook, uncovered, until soft. Meanwhile, beat eggs with fork in large bowl. Stir in 1/2 cup catsup, milk, Worcestershire sauce and salt. Add onion mixture, meat and bread crumbs. Mix until all ingredients are well blended. Shape into a loaf and place in a 9"x5" pan. Spoon on remaining catsup. Bake at 375 degrees for one hour and 15 minutes or until meat thermometer reads 155 degrees. Let stand about 15 minutes before slicing.

Cut shapes from felt; stars, mittens, stockings or hearts, and blanket stitch them in the corner of a flannel blanket...perfect for curling up under on a chilly night!

Tangy Scallops & Pasta

Shelley Turner
Boise, ID

This is perfect for a romantic fireside dinner! Quick to prepare and delicious, I like to serve it with soft bread sticks and a salad.

1-1/2 lbs. scallops
2 T. lemon juice
2 T. fresh parsley, chopped and
    divided
1 t. orange zest
1/2 t. salt

1/8 t. pepper
2 garlic cloves, minced
1 T. olive oil
9-oz. pkg. refrigerated fettuccine

Toss together scallops, lemon juice, one tablespoon parsley, orange zest, salt, pepper and garlic; chill 5 minutes. Sauté scallop mixture in oil for 5 minutes over medium-high heat. Prepare fettuccine according to package directions. Toss scallops with pasta, garnish with remaining parsley.

Spread some neighborhood holiday cheer! Fill a child-size wagon with gifts and goodies for your neighbors; just have the kids pull it from door to door!

Pork Chops & Apples

Mary Hageny
Rhinelander, WI

My grandmother made this recipe often. The flavor is excellent and served with buttered noodles, it's a feast to behold!

8 to 10 baking apples, peeled,
   cored and sliced
2 onions, sliced
6 to 8 pork chops

2 T. oil
2 T. mustard
1/2 c. honey

Layer apples in a 13"x9" pan coated with non-stick spray; top with onions. Brown pork chops in oil and place over onions. Blend together mustard and honey, brush over pork chops. Cover with aluminum foil and bake at 325 degrees for one hour. Serves 6 to 8.

Create a memory box for your children. Paint and stencil a Shaker box, then fill with family photos, childhood grade cards, favorite recipes and special cards and notes saved over the years.

Salmon Patties

Coli Harrington
Delaware, OH

No one will know how easy this dish was to prepare! It's nice if you're looking for something to serve for a special holiday dinner.

1/4 c. red pepper, finely chopped
1/4 c. green onion, finely
   chopped
1 T. lemon juice
1/4 c. mayonnaise

1/4 t. seasoned salt
1 egg, beaten
2 6-oz. cans salmon, drained
1 c. bread crumbs, divided
3 T. butter

In a small mixing bowl, combine red pepper, green onion, lemon juice, mayonnaise and salt; mix well. To mayonnaise mixture, blend in egg, salmon and 4 tablespoons bread crumbs. Roll salmon mixture into 8 balls, roll in remaining bread crumbs then flatten balls into patties. Place butter in a skillet over medium heat until melted. Add patties and cook for about 3 to 4 minutes per side. Makes 8 patties.

Fond memories
and a glowing fire
are kindred
friends...both
delight the heart
and warm the home.

-Anonymous

Italian Sausage & Potatoes

Maureen Baly
Mundelein, IL

*I like to prepare this recipe when my husband and I
have guests. It's wonderfully scrumptious!*

1-1/2 lbs. Italian sausage,
   chopped
10 red potatoes, quartered
1/2 t. pepper
1/2 t. fresh thyme, chopped

1 c. onion, sliced
1 green pepper, chopped
1 red pepper, chopped
14-1/2 oz. can Italian-style
   stewed tomatoes

In 10" skillet, combine sausage, potatoes, pepper and thyme.
Cook over medium-high heat, stirring occasionally, until potatoes are
browned, about 10 minutes. Reduce heat to medium-low. Cover and
cook potatoes until tender, about 10 minutes. Stir in remaining
ingredients. Continue cooking, uncovered, until peppers are
crisp-tender, about 5 minutes. Makes 4 to 6 servings.

Make fragrant fire
starters. Gather together
one-inch cinnamon
sticks, tiny pine cones,
dried orange peel and
cloves; mix well.
Tuck inside a cardboard
tube and wrap the roll with
kraft paper; secure the
ends with jute. Toss several
in a stenciled box
for gift-giving.

Spinach-Mushroom Bake

Lynda Robson
Boston, MA

A hearty dish for those frosty winter days!

2 7-1/2 oz. tubes refrigerated
   buttermilk biscuits
1-1/2 lbs. ground beef
1/2 c. onion, finely chopped
2 eggs
10-oz. pkg. frozen, chopped
   spinach, thawed and drained

4-oz. can mushroom pieces,
   drained
4 oz. Monterey Jack cheese,
   shredded
1/4 c. grated Parmesan cheese
1-1/2 t. garlic powder
salt and pepper to taste
1 to 2 T. butter, melted

Spread biscuits flat and press into a lightly oiled 11"x7" baking dish. Brown ground beef and onion together, drain and set aside. Whisk together eggs, stir in spinach and mushrooms. Add cheeses, garlic powder, salt, pepper and browned beef. Spoon mixture over biscuit crust, drizzle with butter. Bake, uncovered, at 375 degrees for 25 to 30 minutes or until golden. Makes 6 servings.

Make an ice wreath to hang from your outdoor tree branches. Just place greenery and some fresh cranberries inside a round gelatin mold, add about two inches of water, then freeze. Fill the mold completely with water and freeze again. Remove wreath from mold and hang from a length of jute.

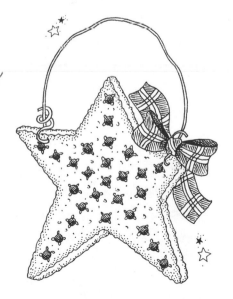

Orange-Pecan Chicken

Erin Doell
Glen Ellyn, IL

Great to make during the busy holiday season. It's ready in less than an hour and is perfect served with wild rice.

1/2 c. butter, melted and divided
4 Cornish game hens
salt and pepper to taste
1/2 c. orange marmalade

1/4 c. orange juice
1 t. cornstarch
1/2 c. chopped pecans

Spread one tablespoon butter equally over hens, season with salt and pepper. Place on a baking sheet and bake at 350 degrees for 25 to 30 minutes, or until juices run clear when skin is pierced. Blend together remaining butter, orange marmalade and orange juice; bring to a boil. Blend together a small amount of cornstarch and water; slowly adding remaining cornstarch until mixture thickens. Slowly add cornstarch mixture to marmalade, stirring constantly; fold in pecans. Place hens in a 13"x9" baking dish. Pour glaze over chicken and bake for an additional 12 to 15 minutes or until glaze begins to brown.

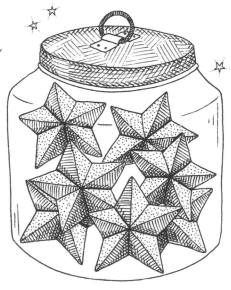

Enjoy a family slumber party! Set up sleeping bags around the tree, have lots of tasty snacks and watch a favorite holiday movie. Before falling asleep, read "The Night Before Christmas" with only the tree lights on.

Ham & Broccoli Casserole

Evelyn Beal
Dover, OH

An easy casserole...let it bake while you're wrapping presents or writing out Christmas cards!

2 10-oz. pkgs. frozen broccoli
2 c. smoked ham, chopped
1-1/2 c. Cheddar cheese,
   shredded

1 c. biscuit baking mix
3 c. milk
4 eggs

Cook broccoli according to package directions. Spread in an ungreased 13"x9" baking dish. Layer ham and cheese over broccoli. Beat remaining ingredients with hand mixer until smooth; slowly pour over cheese. Bake, uncovered, at 350 degrees for one hour. Makes 6 to 8 servings.

This holiday, frame something small and sentimental...several of grandma's buttons, a tiny mitten, a handwritten recipe or worn quilt square. Any of these will make wonderful heart-felt gifts for someone special.

Shrimp Creole

Beverly Mock
Pensacola, FL

So elegant, yet so simple. You'll love serving this special dinner.

1/2 c. onion, chopped
1/2 c. celery, chopped
1 garlic clove, minced
3 T. oil
2 c. canned, chopped tomatoes
8-oz. can Italian-style tomato
   sauce
1-1/2 t. salt
1 t. sugar

1/2 t. chili powder
1 T. Worcestershire sauce
1/8 t. hot pepper sauce
1 t. cornstarch
2 t. water
12 oz. shrimp, peeled and
   deveined
1/2 c. green pepper, chopped
4 c. rice, cooked

Cook onion, celery and garlic in hot oil until tender but not brown. Add tomatoes, tomato sauce, salt, sugar, chili powder, Worcestershire sauce and hot pepper sauce. Simmer, uncovered, for 45 minutes. Mix cornstarch with water; stir into sauce. Cook and stir until mixture thickens. Add shrimp and green pepper. Cover and simmer until done, about 5 minutes, then serve with rice. Makes 4 servings.

Tie three cinnamon sticks together with raffia, then wire them to a greenery garland; repeat along the length of the greenery. Wrap your garland over a window or around a light post for a simple winter welcome.

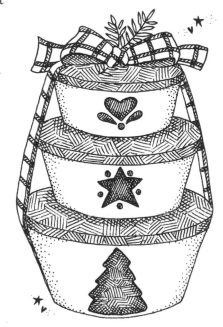

Hearty Holiday Fare

New England Dinner

Robert D'Andrea
Irvine, CA

This classic old-fashioned dinner is great served with warm corn muffins.

5-lb. corned beef brisket
1 garlic clove
8 peppercorns
4 to 5 carrots, peeled and sliced

3 turnips, peeled and quartered
5 potatoes, peeled and quartered
8 onions, peeled and quartered
1 head cabbage, shredded

Place brisket in a large stockpot and cover with cold water. Add garlic and peppercorns; bring to a boil. Reduce heat and simmer brisket 3 to 3-1/2 hours. Remove brisket from broth in stockpot. Add carrots, turnips, potatoes, onion and cabbage to broth and simmer until tender. Return beef to stockpot and heat through. To serve, remove brisket and vegetables and place on a large platter. Makes 6 servings.

You can often find quilt tops that were never sewn together for a great price at flea markets, antique shops or tag sales. Stitch them into a Teddy bear or pillow for a heartwarming gift.

Parmesan Chicken

Linda Patten
Lake Zurich, IL

This delicious chicken can be served over rice, noodles or by itself.

1/2 c. saltine crackers, crumbled
1/2 c. round buttery crackers, crumbled
1/3 c. grated Parmesan cheese
1 stick butter, melted
4 skinless, boneless chicken breasts, cubed

10-3/4 oz. can cream of chicken soup
1 c. milk
8 oz. sour cream

Combine cracker crumbs and Parmesan cheese in medium bowl and mix well. Place melted butter in a small bowl. Dip chicken pieces in melted butter, then roll in cracker mixture. Next, place chicken pieces in a greased 13"x9" baking dish. After you have finished, sprinkle any leftover crumb mixture on top of chicken. Bake at 350 degrees for 30 minutes or until golden brown. Mix soup, milk and sour cream in a large bowl and pour over browned chicken.
Bake 15 minutes longer or until bubbly.
Stir before serving.

Group together lots of tin graters on a tabletop or mantel, you can find them in all sorts of shapes and sizes! Tuck a tea light under each and enjoy their cozy flickering lights.

Italian Beef

Kathee Secor
Orion, IL

Lots of presents to wrap? It will go much faster if you invite friends over for a gift wrapping party! Ask them to bring their gifts, paper, bows and ribbons then spend the afternoon wrapping and chatting about your holiday plans. Add this recipe to your slow cooker the night before and at the day's end, you can enjoy dinner together.

3 to 4-lb. roast
1/2 c. water
1 T. butter
1 garlic clove, minced
1/2 to 1 t. fresh rosemary,
   chopped
1/2 to 1 t. dried oregano
1 green pepper, sliced
1 onion, sliced
10-1/2 oz. can beef broth
12 sandwich buns

Place beef in slow cooker, add water, butter and garlic. Cover and cook overnight on low for 8 hours. Stir in rosemary, oregano, green pepper, onion and broth; continue to cook on low for 8 to 10 hours. When ready to serve, shred and spoon over warm buns.

Blessed are the happiness makers.

—Henry Ward Beecher

Sausage & Red Pepper Quiche

Mary Ann Madalis
Brockway, PA

Serve with a crunchy salad...so delicious and simple!

3/4 lb. sweet Italian sausage, chopped
2 red peppers, finely chopped
9-inch pie crust
1/4 t. salt

1/4 c. Cheddar cheese, shredded
2 T. grated Parmesan cheese
2 eggs
1/2 c. half-and-half
3 T. milk

Place sausage and red pepper in a large skillet. Cook on moderately high heat, stirring constantly, for about 7 minutes; drain. Place pie crust in pie pan, top with sausage and pepper mixture. In a small bowl, mix salt and cheeses together and sprinkle over sausage mixture. Whisk together eggs, half-and-half and milk; pour into pie crust. Bake at 425 degrees for 15 minutes. Reduce heat to 350 degrees and bake an additional 10 minutes.

Everyone can enjoy your favorite Christmas cards and holiday photos under a glass-topped table!

Hearty Holiday Fare

Spiced Cherry Spareribs

Karen Stoner
Delaware, OH

One of our family's favorites...the secret is the sauce!

8 lbs. pork spareribs
21-oz. can cherry pie filling
1/4 c. soy sauce
2 t. spicy brown mustard

1 t. ginger
1 t. Worcestershire sauce
1/2 c. onion, chopped
2 T. olive oil

Cut ribs into sections of 3 each. Place in a Dutch oven and cover with water. Bring to a boil, reduce heat and simmer, covered, for 45 minutes or until tender. Drain and set aside. Using a food processor or blender, purée pie filling and blend with soy sauce, mustard, ginger and Worcestershire sauce. Sauté onion in oil until transparent and add to soy sauce mixture. Pour mixture into a saucepan and simmer, uncovered, for 10 minutes. Place spareribs in a large shallow roasting pan and cover with cherry sauce. Bake at 350 degrees, covered, for 45 minutes. Uncover and bake another 30 to 40 minutes. Makes 8 servings.

Fill an old apothecary jar or hurricane shade with rosehips, cranberries, vintage Christmas balls or cinnamon sticks. Surrounded with greenery, it's a festive centerpiece.

Steak Roll-Up

Carol Shirkey
Canton, OH

Plan ahead...this takes a little extra time to prepare, but it's worth it!

1-1/2 lbs. boneless round steak
1/4 c. onion, chopped
1/4 c. butter, melted
2 c. bread cubes
1/2 c. celery, chopped
1 T. dried parsley flakes
1/2 t. salt
1/2 t. poultry seasoning
1/4 t. pepper
1 c. all-purpose flour
2 T. oil
10-3/4 oz. can cream of
   mushroom soup
1-1/3 c. water
3/4 t. browning sauce

Pound steak to 1/3-inch thickness then cut into 6 pieces. Combine the next 8 ingredients; mix well. Place 1/3 cup onion mixture on each piece of steak; roll up and secure with toothpick; roll each in flour. In a large skillet, brown roll-ups in oil. Combine soup, water and browning sauce; pour over roll-ups. Cover and simmer for 2 hours or until meat is tender; turning occasionally. Makes 6 servings.

Floating candles add charm to a holiday buffet.
Float several in a water-filled yellowware bowl.

Hearty Holiday Fare

Honey-Baked Chicken

Brenda Derby
Northborough, MA

This would be perfect for your Christmas buffet!

3 lb. skinless, boneless chicken
    breasts, chopped
3 to 4 T. butter, melted
4 T. Dijon mustard

2/3 c. honey
1 t. salt
2 t. curry powder

Place chicken pieces in ungreased 13"x9" baking dish. Combine remaining ingredients and pour over chicken. Bake, uncovered, at 350 degrees for one hour to one hour and 15 minutes, basting occasionally until chicken is tender and evenly browned.

Paint a collection of four round boxes to make a clever holiday snowman! Make his hat by painting the top box black with acrylic paint, as well as the lid from the second box. Paint the remaining boxes with white acrylic paint and add a cheery face and any special details you'd like!

Savory Stuffed Chicken

Anna McMaster
Portland, OR

If you like a milder cheese, substitute Gorgonzola or Feta.

1/4 c. onion, chopped
2 T. plus 3 t. unsalted butter, divided
4 egg whites
6 oz. blue cheese, crumbled
1/2 c. bread crumbs
4 boneless, skinless chicken breasts
1/4 c. all-purpose flour

2 garlic cloves, pressed
1 c. chicken broth
3 T. lemon juice
2 T. fresh tarragon, chopped
1 bay leaf
1 c. whipping cream
salt and pepper to taste

Sauté onion in 2 teaspoons butter; set aside to cool. Blend together egg whites, blue cheese, bread crumbs and sautéed onion. Lay chicken breasts out flat and spoon one quarter of the cheese mixture on half of each breast. Fold remaining half of chicken over filling and secure with toothpicks. Sprinkle filled chicken breasts with flour, coating lightly. Heat 2 tablespoons butter in large oven-proof saucepan and brown chicken 2 to 3 minutes on each side. Place saucepan in a 350 degree oven and bake for 35 to 40 minutes or until juices run clear. While chicken is baking, prepare sauce. Sauté garlic in one teaspoon butter. Stir in chicken broth, lemon juice, tarragon and bay leaf. Bring mixture to a boil, then reduce heat and simmer until liquid is reduced by half. Blend in cream, increase heat until mixture boils, reduce heat and continue to simmer until mixture is again reduced by one third. Salt and pepper to taste, discard bay leaf and set mixture aside. When chicken is baked, remove toothpicks and set on a platter. Spoon garlic sauce over each chicken breast before serving.

Out of that frozen mist the snow;
in wavering flakes begins to flow;
flake after flake.

—William Cullen Bryant

Fettuccine with Shrimp & Peppers   *Vickie*

A wonderful and quick-to-prepare seafood dish!

1 lb. asparagus spears, chopped
4 garlic cloves, pressed
1 T. olive oil
1-1/2 lbs. shrimp, peeled and
   deveined
1/3 c. fresh basil, sliced
7-1/4 oz. jar roasted red
   peppers, sliced

1 t. cornstarch
3/4 c. chicken broth
2 T. lemon juice
2 T. white wine
4 c. fettuccine, cooked
pepper to taste

Using a steamer or metal colander placed over a water-filled stockpot, steam asparagus for 5 minutes; set aside. In a separate saucepan, sauté garlic in oil for one minute, add shrimp and continue to cook for 5 minutes or until shrimp turn pink. Remove shrimp from saucepan and set aside. Add asparagus, basil and red peppers to saucepan; heat thoroughly. Whisk together cornstarch and broth; add to basil mixture. Simmer, stirring constantly, for 5 minutes or until mixture thickens. Blend in lemon juice and wine. Toss with pasta and shrimp; sprinkle with pepper. Makes 4 servings.

Stack two or three vintage-style hatboxes on top of each other, then set a cheery potted poinsettia into the top one!

Feta & Shrimp Scampi

Jason Keller
Carrollton, GA

Served with a crisp salad and crusty rolls, this recipe is my favorite for a charming Christmas Eve dinner.

5 garlic cloves, minced
1 t. olive oil
2 28-oz. cans whole tomatoes, drained and coarsely chopped
1/2 c. fresh parsley, chopped and divided

1-1/4 lbs. shrimp, peeled and deveined
1 c. Feta cheese, crumbled
2 T. lemon juice
1/4 t. pepper

In a large saucepan, sauté garlic in oil. Stir in tomatoes and 1/4 cup parsley; simmer 10 minutes. Add shrimp and cook for 5 minutes or until shrimp turn pink. Spoon into a 13"x9" baking dish, top with Feta and bake at 400 degrees for 10 minutes. Top with remaining parsley, lemon juice and pepper before serving.

Handmade touches are perfect at Christmas. Dress up gift tags with old buttons or yo-yos. You can use your cookie cutters as patterns. Just trace around a snowman cookie cutter, cut out and add the finishing touches!

Spanish Noodle Casserole

Joann Bodkin
Gentry, AR

This is one of my favorite recipes; it never fails to bring back wonderful memories of family gatherings.

8-oz. pkg. frozen noodles
1-1/2 lbs. ground beef
1 onion, chopped
1 green pepper, chopped
2 T. oil
15-1/4 oz. can corn

4-oz. can mushroom pieces, drained
3.8-oz. can sliced black olives
8-oz. can tomato sauce
10-3/4 oz. can tomato soup
1/2 lb. colby cheese, grated

Cook noodles according to package directions; drain and set aside. Sauté ground beef, onion and green pepper in oil in a large oven-proof skillet; drain. Add corn, mushrooms, olives, tomato sauce and tomato soup. Stir well, add noodles and sprinkle cheese over casserole. Bake at 350 degrees for 30 minutes or until cheese is bubbly. Makes 8 servings.

Children's woolen mittens or stockings are darling on a tiny greenery wreath!

Stroganoff Casserole

John Alexander
New Britain, CT

*Everyone's favorite, this classic is great for dinner
after a full day of ice skating.*

8 oz. mushrooms, sliced
1 onion, chopped
3 garlic cloves, minced
1 t. oil
1/4 c. dry white wine
10-3/4 oz. can cream of
   mushroom soup

1/2 c. sour cream
1 T. Dijon mustard
1 lb. ground beef, browned
4 c. egg noodles, cooked
Garnish: fresh parsley, chopped

Sauté mushrooms, onion and garlic in oil until onion is translucent; add wine. Reduce heat to medium and simmer for 3 minutes. Remove from heat and blend in soup, sour cream, mustard and ground beef. Spoon noodles into a lightly oiled 13"x9" baking dish. Pour beef and mushroom mixture over noodles and stir to coat. Bake, uncovered, at 350 degrees for 30 minutes or until thoroughly heated. Garnish with fresh parsley. Makes 6 servings.

*Slide a tiny pepperberry wreath around
a chubby pillar candle!*

Hearty Holiday Fare

Homestyle Pot Roast

Liz Plotnick
Gooseberry Patch

*Tender roast beef served with mashed potatoes and glazed carrots;
it's one of the best comfort foods!*

2 T. all-purpose flour
salt and pepper to taste
5-lb. boneless chuck roast
3 T. shortening

1 onion, sliced
1 T. dried thyme
1 c. tomato juice

Sift together flour, salt and pepper; rub over roast. Add shortening to a Dutch oven and melt over medium-high heat. Place roast in Dutch oven and brown on all sides. Reduce heat to medium and add onion, thyme and tomato juice. Simmer, covered, for 3 to 3-1/2 hours turning occasionally. Serves 8 to 10.

A kitchen tree looks perfect decorated with gingerbread men, cookie and biscuit cutters, nutmeg graters, honey dippers, sifters and tin sugar shakers!

Pasta Portabello

Elizabeth Thompson
Aberdeen, NJ

Serve tossed into the pasta of your choice...perfect!

1-1/2 oz. pkg. dried portabello
   mushrooms
3 T. butter
1 onion, coarsely chopped
1 shallot, coarsely chopped
1 garlic clove, minced

1 c. green onions, chopped
1/4 c. soy sauce
1/2 c. red wine
1/4 c. dry sherry
1/2 c. fresh parsley, chopped
salt and pepper to taste

Place dried mushrooms in a medium bowl and cover with hot water. Cover bowl with plastic wrap and soak mushrooms for about 30 minutes. Once the mushrooms are soft, drain in paper towel-lined sieve, reserve the liquid and chop mushrooms. Melt butter in a skillet; add onion, shallot, garlic and green onion; cook until soft, about 5 minutes. Add mushrooms, soy sauce and reserved mushroom liquid; sauté for about 2 minutes on very high heat. Reduce heat, add wine and sherry, simmer until liquid is reduced by half. Add parsley and toss for an additional 2 minutes. Salt and pepper to taste.

Add some Christmas color to an outdoor porch by filling a red enamel pail with inedible osage oranges, also known as hedge apples. Their crisp green color will brighten up any outdoor corner!

Christmas Sideboard

Herb & Cheese Orzo

Linda Karner
Pisgah Forest, NC

Creamy and delicious, a great side dish.

10-1/2 oz. can chicken broth
1 T. herb butter
1 c. orzo

1/2 c. Asiago cheese, shredded
1/8 c. chives, minced
1/4 c. pine nuts, toasted

In a saucepan, bring chicken broth to a boil. Add butter and orzo; cook until orzo absorbs the broth, about 15 to 20 minutes. Add cheese, chives and pine nuts; then serve.

Cheddar Potatoes

Tracy Pamer
Xenia, OH

When your guests tell you how yummy this is, don't tell them how simple it was to prepare!

8 to 10 potatoes, peeled and
    chopped
8-oz. pkg. cream cheese

1-oz. pkg. dry ranch salad
    dressing mix
2 c. Cheddar cheese, shredded

Cover potatoes with water, bring to a boil and cook until tender. Drain; add cream cheese and dry ranch mix. Whip potatoes until fluffy. Place in a 2-quart casserole dish, sprinkle with Cheddar cheese and bake at 350 degrees for 20 minutes.

Enjoy a crisp winter walk at dusk. Afterwards, come home to mugs of chocolatey hot cocoa!

Christmas Sideboard

Broccoli-Noodle Soup

Robbin Chamberlain
Worthington, OH

My children, who are in college, call home to request I make this soup when they know they'll be home for a visit.

1 c. onion, chopped
2 T. butter
6 c. water
6 chicken bouillon cubes
8-oz. pkg. fine egg noodles

6 c. milk
10-oz. pkg. frozen, chopped broccoli
1-1/2 lbs. pasteurized, processed cheese spread, cubed

In large, heavy-bottomed soup pot, sauté onion in butter until transparent. Blend in water and bring to a boil. Add chicken bouillon and noodles. Cook 2 to 3 minutes or until noodles are soft. Stir in milk and turn to low heat. Add broccoli and cheese. Allow to simmer for one hour, uncovered. Do not boil.

There is always a place
for you by my fire,
and though it
may burn to embers,
if warmth and
good cheer are your
desire, the friend of
your heart remembers!

-Anonymous

Raspberry-Applesauce Salad

Tina Wilson
Arlington, WA

*Recently I prepared this salad for my family, and before I noticed,
it was almost all gone! It's definitely a crowd pleaser.*

6-oz. pkg. raspberry gelatin mix
2 c. boiling water
3 c. frozen raspberries

2 c. applesauce
1 c. sour cream
1 c. mini marshmallows

Dissolve gelatin in boiling water. Add raspberries and stir until thawed.
Stir in applesauce. Pour into a glass serving bowl or dish. Chill until
set. Combine sour cream and marshmallows. Spread on top of gelatin.
Chill for 2 hours. Makes 8 to 12 servings.

Frozen Banana Salad

Laura Strausberger
Roswell, GA

Pour into individual muffin cups for single servings!

14-oz. can sweetened condensed
    milk
1/2 c. lemon juice
2 10-oz. pkgs. frozen, sliced
    strawberries

20-oz. can crushed pineapple,
    juice reserved
3 bananas, mashed
16 oz. whipped topping
1 c. chopped nuts

Combine milk, lemon juice, strawberries, pineapple and juice. Stir in
bananas, whipped topping and nuts. Pour into a 13"x9" baking dish;
freeze until solid. When ready to serve, remove from freezer, let thaw
slightly and slice into squares.

*Tuck your jars of layered mixes in an old-fashioned
milk bottle carrier...it's perfect!*

Christmas Sideboard

Eggnog Bread

Megan Brooks
Antioch, TN

Slice and serve with mugs of cocoa after a frosty day of sledding!

2-1/4 c. all-purpose flour
3/4 c. sugar
1 T. baking powder
1 t. salt
1/2 t. nutmeg
1-1/2 c. eggnog

1/2 stick butter, melted
1 egg, beaten
1/2 c. dried apricots, chopped
1/2 c. dried cherries
3/4 c. pecans, chopped

Sift together flour, sugar, baking powder, salt and nutmeg; set aside. In a separate bowl, blend together eggnog, butter and egg. Mix with dry ingredients, stirring until just blended. Fold in apricots, cherries and pecans. Spread batter in a lightly oiled and floured 9"x5" loaf pan. Bake at 350 degrees for 50 minutes to one hour, or until bread tests done. Remove loaf from pan and cool on wire rack.

Write a holiday greeting on a big mug using enamel glass paint. After the paint has dried, fill the mug with chocolate-covered spoons, peppermint sticks or herbal tea bags...a warm and thoughtful winter gift!

Cashew Casserole

Julie McKinney
Apple Valley, CA

I think this is wonderful! If you're watching calories, this is not a low-fat dish; however, it's worth every bite!

2 lbs. ground beef
2 onions, chopped
1/2 lb. American cheese, cubed
2 10-3/4 oz. cans cream of
    mushroom soup
1/2 c. sour cream

2 T. water
1/2 c. mushrooms, sliced
1/2 c. olives, sliced
8-oz. pkg. egg noodles, cooked
1/2 c. cashew pieces
1/2 c. chow mein noodles

Brown ground beef and onions; drain. In separate pan, make sauce of cheese, soup, sour cream and water; add mushrooms and olives. Heat until cheese is melted. In a 13"x9" baking dish layer noodles, ground beef mixture and sauce. Bake at 325 degrees for 35 minutes. Top with cashews and chow mein noodles and return to oven for 10 additional minutes.

A bucket or vintage lunch pail overflowing with a favorite snack will be a welcome gift! Fill it with a variety of nuts, sweet treats or packages of microwave popcorn.

Firecracker Stew

Janie Branstetter
Fairview, OK

This stew is just the thing to warm you up after a cold, snowy day. When my family is in the mood for stew, this is always their first request. My daughter, Tara, gave it the unusual name.

2 lbs. boneless round roast, cubed
1/2 lb. bacon, crisply cooked and crumbled, drippings reserved
1 c. onion, chopped
1/2 c. green pepper, chopped
1/2 c. celery, chopped
1/2 c. carrots, chopped
2 garlic cloves, minced

28-oz. can chopped tomatoes
2 15-oz. cans kidney beans, drained
8-oz. can tomato sauce
2 T. fresh parsley, minced
2 T. chili powder
1 t. salt
1/2 t. cumin
1/8 t. pepper

Brown the beef cubes in bacon drippings for about 5 minutes. Combine browned beef, bacon and remaining ingredients in a slow cooker. Cover and cook on low for 10 to 12 hours or until beef is tender. Makes 8 servings.

Tie cheery red ribbons around bales of hay...presents for Santa's reindeer!

Dilly Coleslaw

Michelle Johnson
Sedalia, CO

A twist on the usual coleslaw recipe...give it a try!

1 cabbage head, shredded
1/2 c. green onion, sliced
1/2 c. red pepper, chopped
3/4 c. dill pickles, chopped
5-3/4 oz. can olives, chopped

1 c. cottage cheese, drained
1/3 c. Italian dressing
1 t. fresh dill weed, snipped
1 t. fresh oregano, chopped
1 garlic clove, minced

Combine cabbage, onion, pepper, pickles, olives and cottage cheese together in a large bowl. In separate bowl, mix together dressing, dill weed, oregano and garlic. Pour dressing mixture over vegetables; toss. Refrigerate at least 4 hours.

Fill lots of old-fashioned canning jars with peppermints or buttons, then tuck a tall dripless taper securely inside each.

Rosebud Dinner Rolls

Donna Cozzens
Gooseberry Patch

This hot roll recipe has been shared in our family many years.
It's truly a complement to any holiday dinner!

1 pkg. active dry yeast
1 c. lukewarm water
1/2 c. sugar
1 stick butter, melted

1 T. salt
2 c. milk, scalded and cooled
3 eggs, beaten
5 c. all-purpose flour, divided

In a large bowl, dissolve yeast in water; let stand until yeast dissolves, about 5 to 10 minutes. Stir sugar, butter, salt and milk into yeast mixture. By hand, or using a heavy-duty mixer, beat eggs and 3 cups flour into yeast mixture. Add enough remaining flour to form a stiff dough. To prepare rosebud rolls, divide dough in half and roll into 2 ropes. Divide each rope into 12 equal pieces and shape each piece into a ball. Place balls 3 inches apart on an oiled baking sheet. Let rise until almost double. Begin at the center of each roll and use a knife to make 5 cuts in the rolls. Bake at 350 degrees for 25 to 30 minutes.

For a cheerful country-style greeting, hang a big wreath on your barn or milk house door!

Garlic Mashed Potatoes

Vickie

If you're looking for a special side dish to take to a holiday potluck, this is the one...you'll get rave reviews!

2 to 4 garlic cloves
2 T. plus 1 t. butter, divided
1 t. olive oil
5 potatoes, peeled and chopped
2 t. salt

1/4 c. sour cream
1/2 c. warm milk
1/4 c. fresh chives, chopped
salt and pepper to taste

To roast garlic, peel each clove and place in a one-pint oven-proof baker. Add one teaspoon butter and olive oil. Bake, covered, at 325 degrees for 45 minutes. The cloves should be golden, but not brown. Remove from oven, cool slightly, then mash with a fork; set aside. In 4-1/2 quart saucepan add potatoes and enough water to cover them. Stir in salt and bring to a boil. Reduce heat to a simmer and continue to cook until tender, about 15 to 20 minutes. Drain then mash with an electric mixer. Add remaining butter and continue to mash until well blended. Add sour cream, milk, chives, garlic and season to taste. Makes 8 servings.

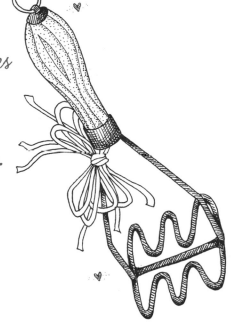

Every house where love abides
and friendship is a guest,
is surely home,
and home sweet home,
for there the heart can rest.

–Henry Van Dyke

Christmas Sideboard

Winnipeg Tortellini Soup

Megan Donahue
Columbia, MO

This wonderful soup was given to me by my friend Brenda, who was stationed with me in the Air Force/NATO exchange program. It's a wonderful soup that reminds me of the warm friendships and memories I made in snowy Canada.

2 lbs. ground Italian sausage, browned and drained
1 zucchini, sliced
1 to 2 yellow squash, sliced
1 onion, diced
1 green pepper, diced
8-oz. pkg. fresh mushrooms, sliced
16-oz. bag frozen, crinkle-cut carrots
10-oz. pkg. frozen, chopped spinach

2 14-1/2 oz. cans chicken broth
2 14-1/2 oz. cans beef broth
2 14-1/2 oz. cans diced tomatoes
15-oz. can tomato sauce
10-3/4 oz. can tomato soup
2 T. dried basil
2 T. dried parsley
2 T. dried oregano
2 to 3 garlic cloves, minced
salt and pepper to taste
2 9-oz. pkgs. cheese tortellini

In a very large soup pot, combine all ingredients. Let simmer for about 4 hours. Add water if necessary to prevent soup from becoming too thick. Check and stir occasionally throughout cooking time.

Roll strips of batting the same way you would to make rag balls, then place them on your Christmas tree...they'll look like snowballs!

Apple-Cranberry Salad

Gail Prather
Bethel, MN

Spoon this festive salad into a glass serving dish; it's so pretty!

2/3 c. sour cream
1/3 c. mayonnaise
2 c. apples, peeled, cored and
   cubed
2 t. lemon juice

1/2 c. dried cranberries
1/2 c. seedless green grapes,
   halved
1/2 c. chopped walnuts
1/2 c. celery, chopped

In a small bowl, stir together sour cream and mayonnaise; set aside. In a large bowl, gently toss apples in lemon juice. Stir in all remaining ingredients. Add dressing; toss to coat. Cover and refrigerate at least one hour before serving. Makes 8 servings.

Slip cranberries on lengths of florist's wire and then shape them into stars...so pretty hanging in each of your windowpanes!

Christmas Sideboard

Holiday Poppy Seed Bread

Sharon Pruess
South Ogden, UT

I like to wrap several loaves of this in pretty bread cloths and give as gifts...perfect for neighbors, teachers or friends.

2-1/2 c. sugar
1-1/2 t. baking powder
2 T. poppy seeds
3 c. all-purpose flour
1 t. salt
2 c. milk, divided

2 t. vanilla extract, divided
1-1/2 t. almond extract
1 c. oil
3 eggs
1 c. powdered sugar

Stir together first 5 ingredients in large mixing bowl. Add 1-1/2 cups milk, 1-1/2 teaspoons vanilla, almond extract, oil and eggs. Beat on medium speed for 2 minutes. Pour into 2 greased and floured 9"x5" loaf pans. Bake in a 350 degree oven for 50 to 55 minutes. Mix remaining milk, vanilla and powdered sugar together until smooth. While bread is still warm, brush with glaze. Allow to cool in pans.

Cover a foam star with white craft glue, then sprinkle on lots of fragrant, dried evergreen needles such as blue spruce or hemlock. They make clever ornaments and party favors!

Au Gratin Potatoes with Ham

Sandra Dodson
Indianapolis, IN

Every time I make this dish, I'm reminded of my mother and the time we spent together as she taught me to cook.

5 potatoes, peeled and thinly
   sliced
2 c. American cheese, cubed
1 onion, chopped

1-1/2 c. smoked ham, cubed
3 t. margarine, divided
salt and pepper to taste
1-1/2 c. milk, scalded

In a greased 2-quart casserole dish, layer the following; potatoes, cheese, onion, ham, one teaspoon margarine, salt and pepper. Repeat layering 2 more times. Slowly pour milk on top; don't stir. Bake, uncovered, at 350 degrees for one hour or until potatoes are tender. Makes 6 servings.

Create a Christmas keepsake
album...add snippets
of wrapping paper,
holiday photos,
special cards and
heart-felt handwritten
notes or letters.

Christmas Sideboard

Clam & Lentil Soup

Claire McGeough
Lebanon, NJ

To create this soup, I just started with a basic recipe, then added lots of our favorite ingredients until we found a combination we loved.

2 c. onions, chopped
1 carrot, grated
1/4 t. dried marjoram
1/4 t. dried thyme
3 T. oil
5 c. water
16-oz. can stewed tomatoes

3 beef bouillon cubes
1 c. dried lentils, rinsed
6-1/2 oz. can chopped clams
1/4 t. paprika
1/4 t. pepper
1/4 c. dry white wine
3 T. dried parsley

In a large soup pot, sauté onions, carrot, marjoram and thyme in oil, stirring often, until lightly browned. Add water, tomatoes, bouillon cubes, lentils, clams, paprika and pepper; bring to a boil. Lower heat, cover and simmer for about one hour. Add wine and parsley; simmer an additional 15 minutes.

Fill a big stoneware bowl with your favorite soup mix, an enamelware ladle, and a package of crackers...sure to be enjoyed on a frosty winter day!

Tropical Island Salad

Kim McGeorge
Ashley, OH

Elegant and delicious, this is perfect for company.

3 T. lemon juice
2 T. honey
4 t. soy sauce
1-1/2 t. fresh ginger, grated
1 garlic clove, minced
1/8 t. white pepper

1/2 c. oil
2 lettuce heads, washed and torn
1/4 c. fresh cilantro, chopped
11-oz. can mandarin oranges, drained
1/4 c. sunflower seeds, toasted

Combine lemon juice, honey, soy sauce, ginger, garlic, pepper and oil; whisking thoroughly. Place lettuce in a salad bowl, add cilantro and arrange orange slices over the lettuce. Sprinkle salad with sunflower seeds. Whisk dressing again and pour over salad, toss and serve. Makes 4 to 6 servings.

Glue buttons of all sizes and colors to a foam wreath; a cheerful holiday greeting!

Christmas Sideboard

Brown Sugar Bread

Amanda Caruso
Oklahoma City, OK

*A Christmas morning favorite...slice and serve with cinnamon
butter or spread on your favorite jam.*

3/4 c. sugar
2 T. butter, divided
1 egg, beaten
3/4 c. milk
2 c. all-purpose flour

2 t. baking powder
1/4 t. salt
1/2 c. brown sugar, packed
cinnamon to taste

Cream sugar and one tablespoon butter. Add egg; mix well. Add milk
and mix again. Sift flour, baking powder and salt; add to egg mixture.
Pour into well greased 9"x5" pan and sprinkle with brown sugar and
cinnamon. Dot remaining butter on top. Bake at 425 degrees for
approximately 25 minutes.

*Remember the
old-fashioned lights
Grandma used to
decorate her tree?
This year, use lots
of colorful,
vintage-style
lights and you'll
capture that
nostalgic feeling.*

Sweet Potato Crunch

Delinda Blakney
Bridgeview, IL

This is a traditional holiday side but the crunchy brown
sugar topping makes this recipe even more tasty!

3 c. sweet potatoes, peeled,
   cooked and mashed
1 c. sugar
1/2 c. plus 3 T. butter, melted
   and divided
2 eggs, beaten
1 T. vanilla extract

1/3 c. milk
1 t. cinnamon
1/2 c. brown sugar, packed
1/4 c. all-purpose flour
1/2 c. chopped pecans

Combine sweet potatoes, sugar, 1/2 cup butter, eggs, vanilla and milk;
mix well. Turn into a greased 2-quart baking dish. Combine remaining
butter, cinnamon, brown sugar, flour and pecans together. Sprinkle
brown sugar mixture over sweet potatoes. Bake at 350 degrees for
25 minutes or until bubbly.

If you love to sew, decorate a tree just for you!
Tie on all kinds of fun sewing notions...a tape
measure garland, spools, thimbles, fabric yo-yos
and pin cushions, would all look terrific!

Christmas Sideboard

Creamy Bacon-Potato Soup

Edwina Gadsby
Great Falls, MT

For me, the combination of potatoes and cheese is a marriage made in heaven! Easy, yet delicious, this is a recipe people request again and again.

4 bacon slices, crisply cooked
   and crumbled, drippings
   reserved
1 onion, chopped
1 t. garlic, minced
1/2 t. dried oregano, crumbled
salt and pepper to taste
6 potatoes, peeled and cubed

2 14-1/2 oz. cans chicken broth
2 T. all-purpose flour
3 c. milk, divided
1 c. smoked sharp Cheddar
   cheese, grated
1 c. sharp Cheddar cheese,
   grated
Garnish: fresh chives, chopped

In saucepan, place one tablespoon bacon drippings, onion, garlic and oregano. Sauté until onions are translucent. Season with salt and pepper, add potatoes and chicken broth. Cover and simmer until potatoes are tender, about 35 minutes then mash with potato masher; don't drain. Blend flour with 1/4 cup milk, stir into potato mixture. Stir in remaining milk and cheeses until smooth. Ladle soup into bowls and garnish with bacon and chives. Makes 4 to 6 servings.

The merry
family gatherings;
the old, the very young,
the strangely lovely
way they harmonize
in carols sung.

-Helen Lowrie Marshall

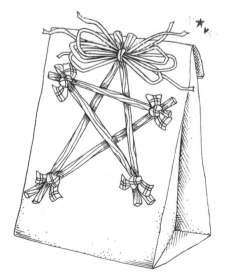

Winter Garden Salad

Jan Fifield
Hemet, CA

Add red peppers for festive color!

1 c. sugar
3/4 c. oil
1/2 c. white wine vinegar
11-oz. can shoepeg corn,
   drained
11-oz. can peas, drained

11-oz. can French cut green
   beans, drained
1 c. celery, finely chopped
1 c. green pepper, finely chopped
1 c. green onions, finely chopped
8-oz. can water chestnuts,
   drained and finely chopped

Mix sugar, oil and vinegar together until sugar is dissolved. Add
remaining ingredients and marinate overnight. Serve chilled.

Wild Rice Salad

Angela Murphy
Tempe, AZ

A great way to use leftover holiday turkey.

4 c. spinach, torn
2 c. turkey, cooked and cubed
2 c. wild rice, cooked
1 onion, chopped

1 c. fresh mushrooms, sliced
20 cherry tomatoes, halved
8-oz. bottle Italian dressing

Combine spinach, turkey, rice, onion, mushrooms and tomatoes.
When ready to serve, toss with dressing.

*Tall tapers tucked inside a sand-filled bucket
cast a warm, soft glow. When your fireplace isn't
in use, just set the lit bucket inside.*

Christmas Sideboard

Christmas Bread

Brenda Carter
Jamestown, NC

I have such fond memories whenever I bake this bread. As a former Air Force wife, I'm reminded of friendships and good times shared across the United States. It simply says "Christmas" to me...the rich smell of cinnamon, a warm kitchen and Christmas carols playing in the background.

18-1/2 oz. box yellow cake mix
3-1/2 oz. pkg. instant pistachio
    pudding mix
4 eggs
1/2 c. oil

1/4 c. water
1 c. sour cream
1/4 c. sugar
1 t. cinnamon

Combine dry cake and pudding mixes, eggs, oil, water and sour cream. Pour into 2 greased 9"x5" loaf pans. In small bowl, mix together sugar and cinnamon. Sprinkle sugar mixture on top of bread mixture; press firmly into bread before baking. Bake at 350 degrees for 40 minutes or until center tests done.

Dip the ends of pretzel rods in melted chocolate, then roll in crushed nuts or holiday sprinkles. Package them in a vintage candy jar for gift-giving!

Honeyed Carrots

Jody Sinkula
Dresser, WI

The sweet taste of these carrots make this a very popular dish!

5 c. carrots, peeled and sliced
1/4 c. butter
1/4 c. honey
2 T. brown sugar, packed

2 T. fresh parsley, chopped
1/4 t. salt
1/8 t. pepper

Place carrots in a saucepan, cover with water and cook just until tender. In a separate bowl, combine butter, honey, brown sugar, parsley, salt and pepper; blend well. Drain cooked carrots, then pour honey mixture over carrots and toss to coat. Place over medium heat until carrots are heated through. If you want to save time and make this dish the night before, place cooked carrots and sauce in a greased 1-1/2 quart casserole dish. Cover with aluminum foil and refrigerate overnight. When ready to prepare, bake at 350 degrees for 20 to 30 minutes. Makes 8 servings.

A candy wreath is a sweet treat! Cut ribbon into 12-inch lengths and curl the ends, then use each ribbon to tie a variety of wrapped candies on a wire wreath form. Continue to tie on candy until you cover the entire form.

Christmas Sideboard

Jalapeño-Chicken Chili

Lisa Case
Clovis, CA

This is an excellent winter warmer after a snowball fight!

2 c. chicken, cooked and cubed
4 15.8-oz. can Great Northern
   beans
1 onion, chopped
1/2 c. red pepper, diced
1/2 c. green pepper, diced
2 jalapeño peppers, seeded and
   finely diced

2 garlic cloves, minced
1-1/2 t. cumin
1/2 t. oregano
3/4 t. salt
1/4 c. water
1/2 t. chicken bouillon
1 to 2 c. salsa

Stir together all ingredients, except salsa and spoon into a slow cooker. Simmer on low heat for 8 to 10 hours or on high heat for 5 hours. Add salsa during last hour. Before serving, stir well to blend.

Fill small fabric bags with pine needles, dried orange peel, tiny pine cones, cloves and cinnamon sticks. Tie closed with ribbon and hang on your door knobs. Each time the door is opened the sachets will release a fresh holiday scent.

Mandarin Orange Salad

Cindy Ziliak
Evansville, IN

*If you're packing the car for a long drive to visit family, just make
this salad before you leave and tuck it into an ice-filled cooler.
By the time you arrive it will be ready to enjoy!*

20-oz. can pineapple chunks,
  drained, juice reserved
15-oz. can mandarin oranges,
  drained, juice reserved
3-oz. pkg. instant tapioca
  pudding mix

3-oz. pkg. instant vanilla
  pudding mix
6-oz. jar maraschino cherries,
  drained
2 bananas, sliced

Pour fruit juices in a 3-cup measuring cup and add enough water to
equal 3 cups; pour into a saucepan. Add dry pudding mixes and cook
over medium heat, stirring constantly until thickened and bubbly;
about 5 to 10 minutes. Remove from heat; cool. Place pineapple,
oranges and cherries in a 2-quart bowl, pour pudding mixture over
fruit and stir to coat. Chill for several hours. Add bananas just before
serving. Makes 6 to 8 servings.

*Deliver a small potted and decorated Christmas tree
to a friend who can replant it outdoors in the spring.
As the tree grows, it will be a constant
reminder of your friendship!*

Christmas Sideboard

Old-Fashioned Raisin Brown Bread

Tiffany Brinkley
Broomfield, CO

This old-fashioned bread is made in a pudding tin then steamed.

1 c. all-purpose flour	1 t. baking soda
1 c. graham flour	1/2 c. molasses
1 c. cornmeal	1-1/2 c. buttermilk
1/2 c. sugar	1/8 c. unsalted butter, melted
1-1/2 t. salt	3/4 c. raisins

Blend together flours, cornmeal, sugar and salt. Stir baking soda into molasses until well blended; add alternately with the buttermilk to dry ingredients; add butter and raisins. Spoon batter into a well-buttered 2-quart pudding mold with a tight fitting lid. Mold should not be more than 3/4 full of batter to allow for expansion. Butter the mold lid and tie down with kitchen string to keep the lid on while the bread is rising. To steam bread, place mold on a metal trivet or canning rack in a large stockpot. Add enough water to come halfway up the sides of the mold. Bring water to a boil, reduce heat to a simmer, cover the stockpot and steam for 3 hours. Check periodically, adding more water if necessary. Carefully remove mold from water and slide out bread to cool.

Bundle up hard-to-wrap gifts like jars or bottles in big squares of homespun or muslin and tie with a raffia bow.

Herbed Rice Pilaf

Jo Ann

I often add shredded chicken or turkey if I want a heartier side dish.

1/4 c. butter
2 c. long-grain rice
1 c. celery, chopped
1/2 c. onion, chopped
4 c. chicken broth

1 t. Worcestershire sauce
1 t. soy sauce
1 t. dried oregano
1 t. dried thyme

Melt butter in a saucepan, stir in uncooked rice, celery and onion. Sauté until rice is lightly browned and the celery and onion become tender. Transfer to a lightly oiled 2-quart casserole dish. Whisk together remaining ingredients and pour over rice mixture. Bake, covered, at 325 degrees for 50 minutes or until rice is tender. Makes 8 servings.

Any dog lover will appreciate this gift!
Fill a galvanized tub, perfect for bath time,
with a bottle of pet shampoo, chew toys, treats,
a grooming brush and coupons for dog sitting.

Christmas Sideboard

Parmesan-Onion Soup

Zoe Bennett
Columbia, SC

A rich and flavorful soup that will warm you to your toes!

3 T. butter, melted
4 c. onions, thinly sliced
1/2 t. sugar
1 T. all-purpose flour
4 c. water

salt and pepper to taste
4 French bread slices, toasted
1/2 c. fresh Parmesan cheese,
   grated

In a large saucepan combine butter and onions, sauté until onions are tender. Stir in sugar and flour and continue to cook for 3 to 5 minutes. Add water and simmer, partially covered, for 30 minutes. Add salt and pepper; blending well. Fill 4 oven-proof bowls with soup, top each with a bread slice and sprinkle generously with Parmesan cheese. Bake in a 400 degree oven until cheese is melted. Serves 4.

Tie a spray of greenery and some wooly mittens to a pair of crossed snow shoes or wooden skis, then sit them by the front door to welcome winter!

Pennsylvania Dutch Potato Salad

Mary Jane Egbert
Phoenix, AZ

The blend of bacon and red potatoes makes this potato salad special!

3 bacon slices, crisply cooked
   and crumbled, drippings
   reserved
3 red potatoes, cooked and
   cubed

1 onion, diced
3 T. vinegar
3 T. sugar
1 egg, beaten

Place bacon, potatoes and onion in a large bowl. In separate bowl, mix vinegar, sugar and egg. When bacon drippings are cool, add vinegar mixture and cook over low heat, stirring, until mix is bubbly. Pour over potato mixture and gently blend.

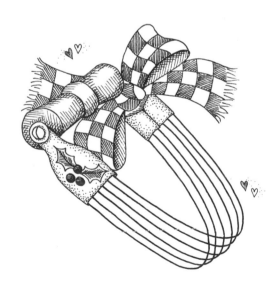

*Antique candy molds in whimsical shapes
such as Santas, trees or reindeer make
charming kitchen decorations!*

Christmas Sideboard

Hot Cross Buns

Sharon Stellrecht
Camona Island, WA

These are great to serve with tea or for breakfast.

2 pkgs. active dry yeast
1/2 c. warm water
1/3 c. sugar
1-1/2 c. milk, scalded and cooled
   to lukewarm
1/2 t. cinnamon
1/4 t. nutmeg
1/8 t. cloves
2 eggs
2 t. salt
2-1/4 t. vanilla extract, divided
6 to 6-1/4 c. all-purpose flour,
   divided
1/3 c. shortening, melted and
   cooled
1 c. raisins
1/2 c. dried currants
2 T. milk
3/4 c. powdered sugar
1 T. water

Dissolve yeast in warm water; add sugar and scalded milk. Beat in spices, eggs, salt and 2 teaspoons vanilla. Stir in 3 cups of flour and beat until batter falls in sheets from spoon. Add shortening and blend in raisins and currants. Gradually add remaining flour, working it well on bread board. Continue kneading until smooth and elastic. Shape into a ball and place in a greased bowl. Grease top of dough. Cover with towel and let rise in a warm place until double. Punch down, shape into a ball, cover and let rest for 10 minutes. Form into biscuit-shaped rolls and place on lightly greased baking pans. Cut a cross into the top of each roll with scissors. Brush tops with 2 tablespoons milk. Let rise, uncovered, in a warm place until double in bulk. Bake in a 400 degree oven for 15 minutes or until golden. Mix together powdered sugar, water and remaining vanilla until smooth. While buns are still warm, make a cross on the top of rolls with frosting. Makes 2-1/2 dozen rolls.

Basil-Topped Tomatoes

Jennifer Guanzon
Meadville, PA

*Recipes that can be prepared quickly are a must during the holiday
season and these tomatoes are ready in less than 10 minutes.*

3 tomatoes
1/4 c. ranch salad dressing
4 T. fresh basil, chopped

4 T. bread crumbs
1/2 c. mozzarella cheese,
   shredded

Slice tomatoes in half, then scoop out and discard half of the pulp
from each tomato half. Spoon dressing equally into each half and
sprinkle with basil. Combine bread crumbs and cheese. Top tomato
halves with cheese mixture. Bake tomatoes 12 inches from broiler
heat for 7 minutes or until cheese is brown and bubbly.

...it was always said
of him, that he knew
how to keep Christmas
well, if any man
alive possessed the
knowledge. May that
be truly said of us,
and all of us!

-Charles Dickens

Christmas Sideboard

Cheesy Vegetable Soup

Belinda Gibson
Amarillo, TX

I think this is the best soup I've ever tasted...it's delicious!

4 10-1/2 oz. cans chicken broth
2-1/2 c. potatoes, peeled and
   cubed
1 c. celery, chopped
1 c. onion, chopped
2-1/2 c. broccoli, chopped
2-1/2 c. cauliflower, chopped
2 10-3/4 oz. cans cream of
   chicken soup

1 lb. pasteurized, processed
   cheese spread, cubed
1 lb. pasteurized, processed
   Mexican cheese spread,
   cubed
1 lb. chicken or ham, cooked
   and cubed

In large soup pot, place chicken broth, potatoes, celery and onion.
Cook for about 20 minutes or until vegetables are tender. Add broccoli
and cauliflower. Cook an additional 10 minutes. Add soup, cheeses
and chicken or ham; simmer until warm.

Use cookie cutters to cut fun shapes from suet
cakes, then hang several in your trees.
The birds will love them!

Cucumber Pasta Salad

Pam Simons
Ashburn, VA

Peas and ham combine to make this creamy holiday salad.

1/2 c. mayonnaise
1/2 c. sour cream
3 T. white vinegar
1 T. honey
1 t. salt
1 cucumber, peeled and seeded

1/2 t. dried dill weed, crushed
2 green onions, chopped
1 t. white pepper
8 oz. fusilli pasta
1 c. peas, cooked
1 lb. smoked ham, cubed

In a food processor or blender, purée together mayonnaise, sour cream, vinegar, honey, salt, cucumber, dill weed, green onions and pepper. Cook pasta according to package directions; drain. Toss the warm pasta with dressing. Stir in peas and ham. Chill until ready to serve.

If you have a historic village in your area, bundle up the kids and go for a visit! Many times the village will have special holiday programs...strolling carolers in vintage costumes, sleigh rides or special recitals in the town hall. You might even find someone roasting chestnuts!

Christmas Sideboard

Cheddar Biscuits with Garlic Butter

Cheri Emery
Quincy, IL

Serve warm with extra garlic butter or pesto on the side.

2 c. biscuit baking mix
2/3 c. milk
1/2 c. Cheddar cheese, shredded

1/4 c. butter, melted
1/2 t. garlic powder

Combine baking mix, milk and cheese with wooden spoon until soft dough forms. Beat vigorously for 30 seconds. Drop by heaping tablespoonfuls onto an ungreased cookie sheet. Bake at 400 degrees for 8 to 10 minutes or until golden brown. In small bowl, blend butter and garlic powder. When biscuits are done, brush with garlic butter, while still on baking sheet. Makes 10 to 12 biscuits.

Make an aged flower pot and fill with spring-blooming bulbs; it's so easy! Turn a new terra cotta pot upside down, rub the outside with buttermilk; let sit in a dark area. After about three weeks it will look like it's been weathering for years!

Oyster Stuffing

Donna Dye
London, OH

A moist and flavorful stuffing recipe I know I can always count on.

2 bread loaves, sliced
2 sticks margarine, divided
1 celery bunch, chopped,
　　reserving tops
2 onions, chopped
1 lb. oysters

48-oz. can chicken broth
4 to 5 dried sage leaves,
　　crumbled
salt and pepper to taste
1 egg

To dry bread, place slices on a baking sheet and bake at 250 degrees for one hour or until slices are dry and feel stale. If available, you could substitute stale bread you may have on hand. Tear dry bread into bite-size pieces and place in a large bowl. Melt 1-1/2 sticks margarine in a large saucepan. Stir in celery and onion and sauté until transparent, about 20 to 25 minutes; set aside. Sauté oysters in remaining margarine until edges begin to curl slightly. Set aside to cool, then chop. Add sautéed celery, onion and oysters to bread; toss gently. Add 2/3 of the can of broth and gently stir to moisten all bread. Add sage, salt and pepper to stuffing; gently stir. Add additional sage if stronger flavor is desired. Whisk egg in a small bowl and pour over stuffing mixture; gently toss. Spoon stuffing into a lightly buttered 3-quart casserole dish and pour remaining broth over top; don't stir. Bake at 325 degrees for one hour. If you'd like to use this recipe to stuff your turkey, spoon 2 to 3 cups of stuffing in the turkey cavity. Do not pack tightly, stuffing swells while cooking. Place turkey in a 325 degree oven and roast for 25 minutes per pound or until a meat thermometer registers 170 degrees in the turkey breast and 185 degrees in the thigh.

Simple gift tags can be made by cutting paper with decorative-edge scissors and gluing assorted buttons around the edges.

Christmas Sideboard

Winter Vegetable Soup

Lynn Williams
Muncie, IN

You can use any of your favorite vegetables for this soup...carrots, red-skin potatoes or cauliflower.

1 onion, chopped
1/4 c. butter
3 sweet potatoes, peeled and chopped
3 zucchini, chopped
1 broccoli bunch, chopped
2 qts. chicken broth

2 potatoes, peeled and shredded
1 t. celery seed
1 to 2 t. cumin
2 t. salt
1 t. pepper
2 c. light cream

Sauté onion in butter until tender. Stir in sweet potatoes, zucchini and broccoli; continue to cook for 5 minutes or until vegetables are crisp-tender. Blend in broth and simmer 3 minutes. Add potatoes, celery seed, cumin, salt and pepper. Simmer 10 minutes or until vegetables are tender. Stir in cream and heat through, but do not bring to a boil. Makes 12 to 16 servings.

Use clothespins to clip different sizes and colors of mittens on jute or clothesline to make a cheery mantel swag!

Best-Ever Green Bean Salad

Nancy DelBuono
West Springfield, MA

At a summer get-together in Otis, my Aunt Nano gave me this recipe which has become a family favorite.

2 garlic cloves, halved
1 lb. fresh green beans, cleaned
    and snapped
1/8 c. olive oil

1/4 c. apple cider vinegar
2 T. red wine vinegar
1 red onion, thinly sliced
salt and pepper to taste

Rub inside of wooden salad bowl with cut garlic. Steam garlic with beans about 10 minutes or until crisp-tender; discard garlic. Drizzle olive oil into wooden bowl coating sides and bottom. Mix in vinegars and add beans, onion, salt and pepper to taste. Toss well and serve at room temperature.

Gently brush your little one's hand in acrylic paint then press on a square of unbleached muslin; let dry. Stitch the fabric into a stocking or pillow...grandparents will love it!

Christmas Sideboard

Holiday Dinner Rolls

Lara Shore
Independence, MO

These rolls are always the highlight of our holiday dinner.
Just serve with apple butter for lots of smiles!

3-1/2 to 4-1/2 c. all-purpose
   flour, divided
3 T. sugar
1 t. salt

2 pkgs. active dry yeast
1 c. milk
1/2 c. water
1/2 c. butter

In a large bowl, thoroughly mix 1-1/2 cups flour, sugar, salt and yeast together. Combine milk, water and 1/4 cup butter in a saucepan and heat over very low heat until liquids are very warm. Butter does not need to melt. Gradually add milk mixture to dry ingredients and beat for 2 minutes at medium speed, scraping bowl occasionally. Add 1/2 cup flour and beat at high speed for 2 minutes. Stir in enough flour to make a soft dough. Turn out onto a floured board and knead until smooth and elastic, about 5 minutes. Place in a greased bowl and turn once to grease top. Cover with towel and place bowl in 98 degree water; let rise for 15 minutes. Divide dough in half, roll into walnut-size balls and place in oiled muffin tins. To make a cloverleaf shape use scissors to cut the top of each roll in an "X". Cover and let rise in warm place for 15 minutes. Melt remaining butter and brush over rolls. Bake at 425 degrees for 12 minutes or until golden brown. Makes 18 rolls.

To have good health
throughout the
next year,
eat an apple on
Christmas Eve.

-Old saying

Take-Along Potatoes

Linda Murdock
Selah, WA

My family's favorite potato dish!

10 to 12 potatoes, peeled and
thinly sliced
1 to 2 onions, sliced
2/3 c. Cheddar cheese, grated
1/2 c. butter, melted

15-oz. can chicken broth
1 T. dried parsley
2 T. Worcestershire sauce
salt and pepper to taste

In a greased 13"x9" pan, layer potatoes, onions and cheese. Pour butter over layered ingredients. Mix together remaining ingredients and pour over layered mixture. Bake, covered, at 425 degrees for 45 to 50 minutes or until potatoes are tender. Uncover, turn off oven and leave baking dish inside for an additional 10 minutes. Makes 10 to 12 servings.

Cranberry Relish

Diane Stegall
Bedford, TX

Cranberry relish with a kick!

2 c. cranberries
1 onion, coarsely chopped
3/4 c. sour cream

2 T. horseradish
1/2 c. sugar

Grind berries and onion in food processor. Add remaining ingredients and mix. Place in an airtight container and freeze until ready to serve. One hour before serving, set in refrigerator to thaw.

Christmas Sideboard

Apple-Bean Bake

Maxine Martin
Beloit, WI

Your kitchen will smell wonderful while this is baking.

4 T. butter
3 c. Granny Smith apples,
    peeled, cored and diced
1 onion, diced
1/2 c. brown sugar, packed
1/2 c. catsup

1 t. cinnamon
1 t. salt
1 T. molasses
17-oz. can lima beans
15-1/2 oz. can kidney beans
16-oz. can pinto beans

Melt butter in a large skillet, stir in apples and onion; cook until tender. Add brown sugar and stir until dissolved. Mix in catsup, cinnamon, salt and molasses, spoon in beans and blend well. Pour into a 2-quart casserole dish. Bake at 400 degrees, uncovered, for about one hour.

Lids of home-canned jams and jellies can be topped with squares of cozy flannel, brown kraft paper or tea-dyed muslin. Secure the fabric with strands of cotton jute tied into a bow. Glue a tiny mitten in the center of the bow for the finishing touch!

Seven Fruit Salad

Connie Bryant
Topeka, KS

The lime dressing is what really makes this fruit salad wonderful!

1/2 c. lime juice
1/2 c. water
1/2 c. sugar
2 peaches, peeled and thinly
   sliced
1 banana, thinly sliced

1 honeydew
1 pt. blueberries
1 pt. strawberries, sliced
1 c. red, seedless grapes, halved
1 kiwi, peeled and chopped

Whisk together lime juice, water and sugar. Stir well until sugar is dissolved. Add peaches and banana; toss to coat. Slice honeydew and use a melon baller to remove the fruit inside. Blend together remaining fruit with honeydew; stir in peach mixture. Refrigerate, covered, for one hour. Makes 8 to 10 servings.

To make a whimsical snowman, sponge paint a pint-size canning jar with white acrylic paint; let dry. Paint on an orange nose and black dots for his eyes and mouth. Add about two inches of sand in the bottom and tuck in a tea light!

Christmas Sideboard

Cranberry-Applesauce Bread

Marion Pfeifer
Smyrna, DE

I like to prepare this bread the day before then serve with our holiday dinner. It's so beautiful when sliced.

2 c. cranberries, chopped
2/3 c. plus 1 T. sugar, divided
1 stick butter, softened
1 egg
1 t. vanilla extract
2 c. all-purpose flour
1 t. baking powder

1 t. baking soda
1 t. cinnamon
1/2 t. salt
1/2 t. nutmeg
1 c. applesauce
1/4 c. milk
1 c. chopped pecans

Toss cranberries with one tablespoon sugar; set aside. Cream butter and remaining sugar together. Beat in egg and vanilla. In a separate bowl, combine dry ingredients. In an additional bowl, combine applesauce and milk. Add flour mixture and milk mixture alternately to the creamed butter; beat well. Stir in cranberries and pecans. Spoon batter into a greased and sugared 9"x5" loaf pan. Bake at 350 degrees for 50 minutes. Cool before serving.

When the heart is right,
the feet are swift.

-Thomas Jefferson

Golden Parmesan Bread Sticks

Melanie Lowe
Dover, DE

Perfect served alongside dinner, or with dipping sauce
if you're hosting a holiday open house.

4 c. bread flour, divided
1 pkg. active dry yeast
1 t. salt
1 T. sugar
1 t. dried rosemary, crushed
1/4 c. grated Parmesan cheese

1/2 t. pepper
1-1/4 c. warm water
2 T. margarine
1 egg white
1 T. water
garlic salt to taste

Blend together 2 cups flour, yeast, salt, sugar, rosemary, cheese and pepper in a heavy-duty mixer. Blend in warm water and margarine; beat for 4 minutes, until a soft dough forms. On a lightly floured surface, knead dough until smooth, adding more flour until dough is no longer sticky. Place dough in a lightly oiled bowl, turning to coat the top. Let rise until double in bulk, about one hour. Divide dough in half and cut each into 12 equal pieces. Roll each piece out until it's approximately 6 inches long; repeat with remaining dough. Place bread sticks on a lightly oiled baking sheet. Whisk together egg white and one tablespoon water, brush over bread sticks. Sprinkle to taste with garlic salt. Let rise until double, then bake at 375 degrees for 15 to 20 minutes or until golden. Makes 24 bread sticks.

Perhaps the best
Yuletide decoration
is being wreathed
in smiles.

—Anonymous

Dessert Sampler

Caramel-Pear Pudding Cake

Margaret Scoresby
Mount Vernon, OH

*A wonderful blend of brown sugar, spice, crunchy pecans
and sweet pears...so warming on a wintry day.*

1 c. all-purpose flour
2/3 c. sugar
1-1/2 t. baking powder
1/2 t. cinnamon
1/4 t. salt
1/8 t. cloves
1/2 c. milk

4 pears, peeled, cored and
   chopped
1/2 c. chopped pecans
3/4 c. brown sugar, packed
3/4 c. boiling water
1/4 c. butter

Mix flour, sugar, baking powder, cinnamon, salt and cloves. Stir in
milk until smooth. Fold in pears and pecans. Transfer batter to an
ungreased 2-quart casserole dish. Mix together brown sugar, water
and butter. Blend well and pour over batter; don't stir. Bake at
375 degrees for 45 minutes. Makes 8 servings.

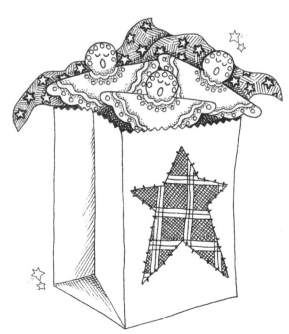

*Add a sweet holiday
fragrance to your
crackling fire...just
toss in a handful of
dried mint leaves,
orange peel or
cinnamon sticks!*

Dessert Sampler

Maple-Spice Pecan Pie

Sharon Shepherd
Terre Haute, IN

The sweet maple flavor makes this pie special.

2 9-inch pie crusts
3 eggs
3/4 c. brown sugar, packed
1 c. maple syrup
3 T. butter, melted

1 T. lemon juice
1 t. vanilla extract
3/4 t. nutmeg
1/4 t. salt
1-1/2 c. chopped pecans

Place each pie crust in a pie pan; set aside. In a large bowl, whisk eggs and brown sugar. Add maple syrup, butter, lemon juice, vanilla, nutmeg and salt; whisk to blend. Add nuts and pour into pie crusts. Bake at 450 degrees for 10 minutes. Lower to 350 degrees and bake an additional 30 to 35 minutes. Makes 2 pies.

The more it snows,
the more it goes,
the more it goes
on snowing.
And nobody knows
how cold my toes,
how cold my toes
are growing!

-A.A. Milne

Chocolate Chip Squares

Linda Zell
Delavan, WI

*Mom probably made hundreds of these delicious bar cookies
over the years! Any time my sister and I had to bring
a treat to a party, we asked her for these.*

1-1/2 c. brown sugar, packed
   and divided
1 c. plus 2 T. all-purpose flour,
   divided
1/2 c. margarine, softened
2 eggs, beaten

2 t. baking powder
1 t. vanilla extract
6-oz. pkg. chocolate chips
1/4 t. salt
1/2 to 1 c. chopped walnuts

Mix together 1/2 cup brown sugar, one cup flour and margarine. Press
into bottom of 13"x9" pan. Bake at 350 degrees for 10 to 15 minutes.
or until lightly browned . Mix together remaining ingredients and pour
over hot crust. Bake at 350 degrees for 20 to 25 minutes. When cool,
cut into small squares. Makes 48 bars.

*A festive Santa hat is a terrific place
to tuck in all the greeting cards you receive!*

Dessert Sampler

Fabulous Fruit Pizza

Mary Ann Clark
Indian Springs, OH

You can top this with any of your favorite fruit. It's so pretty!

2-1/2 c. sugar, divided
1/2 c. butter
1 egg
1 t. vanilla extract, divided
1 t. baking powder
1/2 t. baking soda
6 T. buttermilk
3 to 4 c. all-purpose flour
3 T. cornstarch
1/8 t. salt
3/4 c. water

1 c. orange juice
1/4 c. lemon juice
8-oz. pkg. cream cheese
5 to 6 kiwi, peeled and sliced
2 to 3 bananas, sliced
1 pt. fresh strawberries, sliced
11-oz. can mandarin oranges, drained
2 c. canned pears, drained and sliced
1/2 c. blueberries

Cream one cup sugar and butter until smooth. Add egg, 1/2 teaspoon vanilla and baking powder; continue beating. In a separate bowl, combine soda and buttermilk; add to creamed mixture. Stir in flour until soft dough forms, adding enough so that the dough is not sticky. Divide dough in half. Wrap one half in plastic zipping bag and freeze for future use. Roll remaining half into a greased 12" pizza pan. Bake at 400 degrees for 10 minutes, or until top becomes slightly browned; cool. In small saucepan, combine one cup sugar, cornstarch and salt. Add water, orange juice and lemon juice. Cook and stir on medium heat until mixture becomes thick and bubbly. Remove from heat. Cool to room temperature. Mix cream cheese with 1/2 cup sugar. Add remaining vanilla. Spread mixture on crust. Arrange fruit on crust in circles, beginning with kiwi fruit on outside edge and overlapping fruit. Continue circling with bananas, strawberries, oranges and pears finishing with a small circle of kiwi or strawberries in center using as much fruit as possible. Randomly place blueberries on top of other fruits. Carefully spoon sauce over top of fruit. Cut into 8 large pieces; serve.

For pretty placecards, use silver or gold markers to write names on magnolia or holly leaves.

Buttery Chocolate-Nut Toffee

Lynn Blamer
Bangor, MI

*Fill a vintage jar with this toffee, then tie on a homespun
bow...a tasty gift from your kitchen!*

1 c. butter
1 c. sugar

6-oz. pkg. semi-sweet chocolate
chips
1/4 c. chopped walnuts

In a 2-quart saucepan, combine butter and sugar. Cook over low heat,
stirring occasionally, until a small amount of mixture dropped into
ice water forms a brittle strand or a candy thermometer reaches
300 degrees. Spread on wax paper-lined jelly roll pan. Sprinkle
chocolate chips over hot candy; let stand 5 minutes. Spread melted
chocolate evenly over candy; sprinkle with walnuts. Cool completely
and break into pieces.

*Pile fir sprigs, cookie cutters and pepperberries
in a large yellowware or wooden dough bowl to
make a charming country centerpiece.*

Dessert Sampler

White Chocolate Fudge

Jo Ann

Just right for tucking in holiday tins!

8-oz. pkg. cream cheese, softened
4 c. powdered sugar

1-1/2 t. vanilla extract
12 ozs. white chocolate
3/4 c. chopped walnuts

Cream together cream cheese, sugar and vanilla until smooth. Melt chocolate in a double boiler, then stir into cream cheese mixture. Fold in walnuts and spread into a greased 8"x8" baking pan. Chill until ready to serve and cut into squares.

Caramel Corn

Jana Warnell
Kalispell, MT

My mother would make batch after batch of caramel corn to give out as gifts during Christmas.

2 c. brown sugar, packed
1 c. butter
1/2 c. corn syrup

1 t. vanilla extract
20 c. popped popcorn

Combine first 3 ingredients in a saucepan and bring to a boil; boil for 5 minutes. Remove from heat and stir in vanilla. Pour over popcorn; stirring until thoroughly blended. Spoon on a baking sheet and bake at 250 degrees for one hour, stirring every 15 minutes.

A family is a circle of friends who love you.

-Unknown

Dark Chocolate Caramels

Audrey Lett
Newark, DE

Chewy and so chocolatey!

1-1/2 c. whipping cream
1-1/4 c. honey
8 oz. bittersweet chocolate,
    finely chopped
1/2 c. sugar

1/2 c. brown sugar, packed
2 T. unsalted butter, softened
1 t. vanilla extract
1 T. oil

Blend together cream, honey, chocolate, sugar and brown sugar. Over medium heat, bring mixture to a boil. Continue cooking syrup, stirring constantly, until the temperature reaches the hard ball stage, 250 to 268 degrees on a candy thermometer. Remove saucepan from heat and quickly stir in butter and vanilla. Line an 8"x8" metal baking pan with aluminum foil, then coat aluminum foil with oil; pour in caramel mixture. Set aside to cool for 2 hours. When cool, slide aluminum foil from baking pan. Cut into squares with an oiled knife. Store squares between sheets of wax paper in a container with a tight fitting lid.

Sprigs of evergreen, tiny pine cones, rosehips and cinnamon sticks tucked inside a quart-size canning jar can become a quick and easy gift! Just set a votive holder inside the jar rim and slip in a tea light.

Dessert Sampler

Buckeye Bars

Aisling Reynolds
Columbus, OH

Sometimes I substitute white chocolate or butterscotch chips for a different taste.

1 stick butter
1-1/2 c. graham crackers, crushed
14-oz. can sweetened condensed milk

12-oz. pkg. semi-sweet chocolate chips
10-oz. pkg. peanut butter chips

Melt butter in 13"x9" glass baking dish. Spread graham cracker crumbs over butter. Pour sweetened condensed milk over crumbs, top with chocolate and peanut butter chips. Press down firmly with spoon. Bake at 325 degrees for 25 to 30 minutes.

Snowman Brownies

Kathy Grashoff
Ft. Wayne, IN

A fun after-school treat!

21-1/2 oz. pkg. fudge brownie mix

1/2 c. mini marshmallows
4-1/4 oz. tube black icing

Prepare brownie mix according to package directions and spread in a 13"x9" pan. Place marshmallows on brownie batter in the outline of a snowman; bake as directed on box of mix. Cool brownie in pan on a wire rack. When completely cooled, add a decorating tip to the tube of icing and pipe on arms, a hat, eyes and a mouth. Makes 24 servings.

A red sugar bucket looks cheerful filled with green Granny Smith apples!

Coffee-Toffee Cookies

Mary Steiner
West Bend, WI

I always make these cookies during the Christmas holidays;
they're a hit for the annual cookie exchange!

1 T. instant coffee granules
1 t. vanilla extract
2 sticks butter, softened
1-1/4 c. sugar

1/2 t. baking powder
1 egg
2-1/2 c. all-purpose flour
3/4 c. toffee chips

Stir coffee and vanilla in a cup until the coffee dissolves into the vanilla. Beat butter, sugar and baking powder together in a large bowl with electric mixer until fluffy, blend in egg and coffee mixture. Beat in flour gradually. Divide dough in half and roll each half on a lightly floured surface into about a 9-inch log. Wrap each log in plastic wrap and refrigerate about 4 hours or until firm. Cut in 1/4-inch slices and place on a greased baking sheet about 2 inches apart. Place 1/2 teaspoon toffee chips on top of each cookie, press in lightly. Bake at 350 degrees for 10 to 12 minutes. Makes about 4 dozen.

Give cookie cutters a vintage look by brushing them with black acrylic paint thinned with a little water; let dry. Apply a coat of weathering paint, found at craft stores, and when it's dry you'll have a collection of antique-looking cookie cutters perfect for hanging on the tree!

Dessert Sampler

Chocolate Chip Macaroon Bars

Sheryl Thomas
Potterville, MI

Tuck these in an old-fashioned cookie jar for gift-giving.

1/2 c. butter
1 c. plus 2 T. all-purpose flour, divided
1-1/2 c. brown sugar, packed and divided
2 eggs

1/4 t. salt
1 c. chopped pecans
1-1/2 c. flaked coconut
1 t. vanilla extract
1 c. chocolate chips

Mix together butter, one cup flour and 1/2 cup brown sugar. Pat into the bottom of a 13"x9" greased baking pan. Bake at 325 degrees for 15 minutes. In medium bowl, blend together remaining flour and brown sugar, eggs, salt, pecans, coconut, vanilla and chocolate chips. Spread mixture onto baked crust. Bake for an additional 25 minutes. Cut into bars when cool.

*It's Christmas time and once again
the world repeats the story,
of peace on earth, good will to men
and children sing the glory.*

—Mirla Greenwood Thayne

Magic Window Cookies

Anne Tufo
Heath, TX

My kids love to make these!

3/4 c. shortening
1 c. sugar
2 eggs
1 t. vanilla extract

2-1/2 c. all-purpose flour
1 t. baking powder
1 t. salt
6 pkgs. hard candy, crushed

Mix shortening, sugar, eggs and vanilla. Blend in flour, baking powder and salt. Cover and chill for at least one hour. Roll dough to 1/8-inch thick on lightly floured cloth-covered board. Cut dough with cookie cutters that have a cut-out in the middle or if using regular cookie cutters, cut out center of dough with mini cookie cutters. Place cookies on an aluminum foil-covered baking sheet. Place crushed candy in the cookie cut-outs, just fill cut-outs until candy is level with the dough. Bake cookies at 375 degrees for 7 to 9 minutes. Makes 3 or more dozen depending on size of cut-outs.

Use a pastry tube to pipe icing names on cut-out cookies...angels, snowflakes or reindeer will all make tasty place markers!

Dessert Sampler

S'more Bars

Jan Ertola
Martinez, CA

A favorite fireside treat becomes a cookie...you'll love these!

1/2 c. butter, softened
1/2 c. sugar
1 egg
1 t. vanilla extract
3/4 c. graham crackers, crushed
3/4 c. all-purpose flour

1/4 t. salt
1 t. baking powder
3 1-1/2 oz. chocolate candy
    bars
7-oz. jar marshmallow creme

In a large mixing bowl, cream butter and sugar until fluffy. Beat in the egg and vanilla extract. Add crushed graham crackers, flour, salt and baking powder; beat until well mixed, scraping the sides of the bowl. Spoon half of the dough into a greased 8"x8" baking pan and spread evenly. Break chocolate bars into pieces and arrange over the dough. Spread a layer of marshmallow creme over the chocolate. Flatten the remaining dough into pancake shapes and lay over marshmallow creme. Bake at 350 degrees for 30 minutes or until golden brown. Allow to cool and cut into 16 squares.

Let us keep Christmas beautiful...that it shall not be just a day, but last a lifetime through.

-Garnett Ann Schultz

Grandma's Apple Pie

Tina Knotts
Gooseberry Patch

An old-fashioned favorite...bake it for someone special.

1 c. sugar
3 c. water
1 t. cinnamon
1/8 t. salt
1/2 stick margarine
2 T. cornstarch

8 to 10 apples, peeled, cored
  and sliced
9-inch pie crust
1/4 c. brown sugar, packed
3/4 c. all-purpose flour
1/4 stick butter

In large saucepan, mix together sugar, water, cinnamon, salt, margarine, cornstarch and apples. Heat on medium high until thickened and apples are soft. Pour apple pie filling into pie crust. Mix together brown sugar, flour and butter with fork until crumbs form. Sprinkle on top of pie filling. Bake at 400 degrees for 15 to 20 minutes.

Set empty pie tins in a wire pie rack, then add two or three tealights to each tin. Surround the tealights with bright cranberries, tiny hemlock cones, sumac berries, cinnamon sticks, star anise and whole cloves...a simple and natural centerpiece.

Dessert Sampler

Old-Fashioned Gooseberry Pie

Ronald Smith
Washington, IN

This is just like the delicious gooseberry pies Mother used to make.

2 9-inch pie crusts
3 c. gooseberries, washed and
    stemmed
1 T. all-purpose flour

1 to 1-1/2 c. sugar
1 T. butter
1 egg

Line pie plate with one crust and fill with gooseberries. Mix together flour, sugar, butter and egg. Carefully spread this mixture over the gooseberries. Place top crust on pie. Pierce crust with fork. Bake at 400 degrees for 35 minutes or until crust is golden.

Sweet Orange Delight

Joy Nenonen
Watersmeet, MI

Cool and refreshing!

2 11-oz. cans mandarin
    oranges, drained, juice
    reserved
20 marshmallows

3-oz. pkg. orange gelatin mix
8-oz. pkg. cream cheese
8 oz. whipped topping

Pour reserved juice in a 2-cup measuring cup and add enough water to make 2 cups of liquid. Heat to boiling; add marshmallows. Stir to melt; add dry gelatin, mix and let cool. Mash oranges, mix in with cream cheese then add to cooled marshmallow mixture. Fold in whipped topping and chill until ready to serve.

Moravian Sugar Cake

Lisa Burwell
Kinston, NC

My mother's version of this easy-to-make cake.

1/2 c. potatoes, mashed, potato
   water reserved
2 pkgs. active dry yeast
1/2 c. sugar
1/4 t. salt
2 eggs

1 c. butter, divided
2-3/4 c. all-purpose flour,
   divided
1 c. brown sugar, packed
2 t. cinnamon

In a large, warm mixing bowl, sprinkle yeast over 1/2 cup warm potato water; beat well. Add sugar, salt and eggs. Melt 1/2 cup butter in hot potatoes, beat well and add to yeast mixture. Add half of flour and beat hard for 3 to 5 minutes. Add remaining flour and mix well with wooden spoon. Place in greased and covered bowl and refrigerate at least 12 hours. Divide dough in half and spread thinly with floured fingers into two, 13"x9" pans. Let rise until double, about 2 hours. Coat your thumbs with flour, then make holes randomly in dough. Fill holes with mixture of brown sugar, remaining butter and cinnamon. Bake at 400 degrees for about 15 to 20 minutes.

It's food too fine for angels; yet, come, take and eat thy fill! It's heaven's sugar cake.

-Edward Taylor

Dessert Sampler

Cape Cod Cranberry Pie

Dianne Sullivan
East Sandwich, MA

This gets rave reviews here in cranberry country!

2 c. cranberries
1-1/2 c. sugar, divided
1/2 c. chopped walnuts
1/2 c. butter, melted

1 c. all-purpose flour
4 T. oil
2 eggs
2 t. vanilla extract

Spray a 9" deep dish pie pan with non-stick spray. Add cranberries, sprinkle with 1/2 cup sugar and walnuts. Mix remaining ingredients together with wire whisk. Pour over cranberries in pie plate. Bake at 325 degrees for 45 minutes or until brown.

Make a yummy cookie garland!
Bake a batch of sugar cookies, don't forget
to put a hole in the top before baking.
When they've cooled, slip a ribbon through the holes.
String cranberries and popcorn on a length of
fishing line, then tie the cookies along your garland!

Walnut-Chip Pie

Ann Fehr
Trappe, PA

I remember my mother making this almost every week!

1 c. sugar	1 c. chopped walnuts
1/2 c. all-purpose flour	1 c. chocolate chips
2 eggs	1 t. vanilla extract
1 stick butter, melted and cooled	9-inch pie crust

Mix first 7 ingredients together and pour into pie crust. Bake at 325 degrees for one hour. Makes 8 to 10 servings.

Cranberry-Apple Pudding

Marie Brandt
Cold Brook, NY

This recipe is special to me because it always brings to mind the sweet aroma that filled Grandma's house as she was baking it.

4 apples, peeled, cored and thinly sliced	juice and zest of one orange
1 c. cranberries	1/2 t. apple pie spice
1/4 c. raisins	1 c. milk
	1 c. bread crumbs

Combine all ingredients and place into a 2-quart glass baking dish. Bake, covered, at 350 degrees for 40 to 50 minutes or until firm in the center. Serve warm. Makes 4 to 5 servings.

Make a quick Williamsburg-style wreath!
Use florist's pins to secure lady apples,
lemons and clementines to a foam wreath.
After you've covered it completely,
fill in empty spaces with greenery.

Dessert Sampler

Southern Pecan Pralines

Juanita Williams
Jacksonville, OR

On a family trip to see our son graduate, we traveled through Georgia and South Carolina. While touring the plantations, I found a wonderful book that shared Christmas traditions of the old South. These wonderful pralines are reminiscent of that simpler time.

1-1/2 c. brown sugar, packed	1 c. milk
1-1/2 c. sugar	1 t. vanilla extract
3 T. corn syrup	1-1/2 c. chopped pecans

Combine sugars, corn syrup and milk in a heavy 4-quart saucepan. Cook over medium heat, stirring constantly, until the mixture comes to a boil. Turn the heat to low and continue stirring until a little of the mixture dropped into cold water forms a soft ball or mixture reaches 234 to 240 degrees on a candy thermometer. Remove from heat and let stand for 10 minutes. Stir in the vanilla and beat for 2 minutes, using a wooden spoon. Add pecans and stir until creamy. Drop by spoonfuls onto wax paper to make patties about 2-1/2 inches in diameter. Let the pralines stand until cold and firm, then peel from the wax paper. Makes 3 dozen.

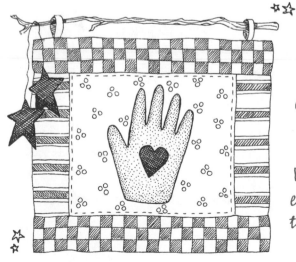

Instead of sending holiday cards, exchange signed and dated quilt squares with friends. When you've collected enough squares, stitch them together to make a friendship quilt.

Brownie Treat

Valerie Marsh
Sandy, UT

A rich and chewy chocolate treat!

1/2 c. plus 1 T. butter, divided
1 c. sugar
1 t. vanilla extract
2 eggs
3 1-oz. squares unsweetened
    chocolate, melted and
    divided

1/2 c. all-purpose flour
3 c. mini marshmallows
2 T. warm water
1 c. powdered sugar

Cream together 1/2 cup butter, sugar and vanilla; beat in eggs.
Blend in 2 ounces chocolate and flour. Bake in a greased 9"x9" pan at
325 degrees for 30 to 35 minutes. Arrange marshmallows on top of
brownies. Return to oven for about 3 minutes or until marshmallows
start to melt. Remove from oven and set aside. In saucepan, melt
remaining chocolate and butter over low heat; blend in warm water.
Remove from heat and pour in powdered sugar. Mix well and drizzle
chocolate over marshmallow topping. Cool before cutting into squares.

*Sponge paint a frosty
scene on the glass of
a recycled window
frame...a tree,
snowman or Santa.
After the paint dries,
attach hooks on the top
and hang your window
where light can
shine through it.*

Dessert Sampler

Marbled Pumpkin Cheesecake

Kim Schwarz
Howard, OH

This looks so pretty on a holiday buffet table.

3/4 c. gingersnaps, crushed	4 eggs
3/4 c. graham crackers, crushed	1-lb. can pumpkin
1-1/4 c. sugar, divided	1/2 t. cinnamon
1/4 c. butter, melted	1/4 t. ginger
2 8-oz. pkgs. cream cheese	1/4 t. nutmeg

In bowl, combine gingersnap and graham cracker crumbs with 1/4 cup sugar and butter. Press into the bottom of a 9" springform pan. Bake at 350 degrees for 5 minutes. In a mixing bowl, beat cream cheese until smooth. Gradually add one cup sugar; beat until light. Add eggs, one at a time, beating well after each. Transfer 1-1/2 cups of cream cheese mixture to a separate bowl and blend in pumpkin and spices. Pour half of pumpkin mixture into prepared pie crust. Top with half of cream cheese mixture. Repeat layers using remaining pumpkin and cream cheese mixtures. Using a table knife, cut through layers with uplifting motion in 4 to 5 places to create marbled effect. Bake at 350 degrees for 45 minutes without opening oven door. If you place a shallow pan of water on a lower rack of the oven while you bake the cheesecake, the top won't crack. Turn off oven and let cake stand in oven for one hour. Remove and chill.

A good conscience is a continual Christmas.

-Benjamin Franklin

Crazy Quilt Pie

Anne Tufo
Heath, TX

*I think this must be the easiest pie in the world to bake and
its wonderful taste will rival any custard pie!*

2 c. milk
4 eggs
1/2 c. all-purpose flour
1 c. flaked coconut

1 c. sugar
1 stick butter
1/2 t. salt
1 t. vanilla extract

Place all ingredients into a blender. Turn the blender on medium speed
and count to ten. Pour into a 9" deep dish pie pan. During the baking
process the flour drops to form the crust and the remaining ingredients
form the filling. Bake at 350 degrees for 45 minutes.

Small cheer and great welcome make a merry feast!

-William Shakespeare

Dessert Sampler

Mint-Chocolate Bars

Sarah Ercanbrack
Alpine, UT

I like to cut these into tiny squares for nibbling at holiday parties!

16-oz. can chocolate syrup
1 c. sugar
2 sticks plus 6 T. margarine,
   divided
4 eggs
1 c. all-purpose flour
3 t. vanilla extract, divided

1/2 t. butter flavoring
2 c. powdered sugar
1 t. peppermint extract
2 T. milk
1 to 2 drops green food coloring
2/3 c. chocolate chips

Mix together chocolate syrup, sugar and one stick creamed margarine. Add eggs, one at a time, then stir in flour, one teaspoon vanilla and butter flavoring. Pour into a 13"x9" baking pan. Bake at 350 degrees for 20 minutes. In separate bowl, mix together powdered sugar, one stick margarine, peppermint extract, milk and green food coloring. Spread over brownies and refrigerate overnight. In a saucepan, melt chocolate chips, remaining margarine and remaining vanilla. Spread over chilled bars and refrigerate. Cut into squares.

The cold was our pride,
the snow was our beauty.
It fell and fell,
lacing night together
in a milky haze.

-Patricia Hampl

Chocolate-Buttermilk Cake

Kris Lammers
Gooseberry Patch

*No one will ever guess the secret ingredient of
this tasty devil's food cake!*

2-1/2 c. all-purpose flour
1-3/4 c. brown sugar, packed
1 t. baking powder
1 t. baking soda
1 t. cinnamon
8 1-oz. squares unsweetened
   chocolate, melted and
   divided

1 c. buttermilk
1 c. green tomatoes, puréed
3/4 c. plus 3 T. butter, softened
   and divided
2 eggs
1 T. orange zest
1-1/4 c. powdered sugar
3 T. hot water

Stir together flour, brown sugar, baking powder, baking soda
and cinnamon; set aside. Blend together 4 ounces chocolate,
buttermilk, tomatoes, 1/4 cup butter, eggs and orange zest. Using
an electric mixer, blend until thoroughly combined. Pour into a
greased and floured 13"x9" baking pan and bake at 350 degrees for
35 to 40 minutes or until toothpick inserted near the center comes out
clean. Let cake cool in pan. Combine remaining chocolate and butter;
stir in powdered sugar and blend. Add hot water if glaze is too thick.
Drizzle over cake before serving.

*If you have urns
on your porch, fill
them with greenery
then set a pineapple
in the middle...a
very old-fashioned
welcome symbol!*

Christmas in the Country

Country-Style Candles

Becky Sykes
Gooseberry Patch

Light the way to your home with country-style candleholders!

canning jars of different sizes
16-gauge wire
sand, small gravel or cat litter

3 2 or 3-inch pillar candles
wire cutters

Gather together several sizes of glass canning jars. Use pliers to twist a loop at each end of a length of 16-gauge wire, this will be your handle. Wrap another piece of wire around the lip of your canning jar, slipping it through the 2 loops of the handle. Twist the ends of the wire around the jar lip and cut off any excess with wire cutters. Repeat with your remaining glass jars making the handle on each a different length. To keep a candle from tipping over, fill the bottom of each jar with about one inch of cat litter, sand or gravel, then tuck a 2 or 3-inch pillar candle securely inside. Hang 2 or 3 on a shepherd's crook. They'll look great along your walkway, lighting the porch steps or scattered throughout your garden.

Hang up tin can luminarias! Freeze water in soup cans then use a hammer and awl to tap in a design. Don't forget to add two holes at the top, on opposite sides, to slip your wire through for hanging! Let the water thaw, place sand and votives in, then set along your steps.

Christmas in the Country

Farmhouse Table

Beth Kramer
Port Saint Lucie, FL

You could keep this farmhouse table out year 'round, but it's especially pretty during the holidays!

6 4 gal. crocks
crumpled newspaper

favorite winter decorations
custom cut piece of glass

To make the base of your table, line up 6 crocks in a rectangle. If you're filling them with something small, such as dried oranges, you may want to partially fill the crock with crumpled newspaper so you don't have to use quite so many dried oranges. Fill each crock with something different...evergreen sprigs, holly branches, pine cones, dried apples and oranges, cinnamon sticks, woolen mittens, vintage ornaments or even wrapped presents! To complete your farmhouse table, top the crocks with a custom cut piece of glass. By gently removing the glass top, you can change the contents of the inside anytime throughout the holidays

*...joyous days
and jolly nights
and merry
Christmas times!*

-Oliver Wendall Holmes

Snowflake Hurricanes

Carrie O'Shea
Marina Del Ray, CA

Set several of these along your buffet table.

Con-Tact® paper
glass hurricane shades

rubber gloves
etching cream

Cut out a snowflake pattern on a sheet of Con-Tact® paper; set the snowflake aside. Using the snowflake "background" piece, gently peel the backing from the Con-Tact® paper and position it on a glass shade. If you want some of the glass to show through your snowflake, cut out little shapes from Con-Tact® paper, remove the backing and place them on the glass inside your snowflake. Wearing a pair of rubber gloves, apply etching cream to the open areas of the snowflake, according to the manufacturer's instructions on the jar. Let dry for 15 minutes. Rinse your glass shade under warm running water to remove the cream and Con-Tact® paper, then wash with soap and water; dry thoroughly. Tuck a candle or votive inside and enjoy!

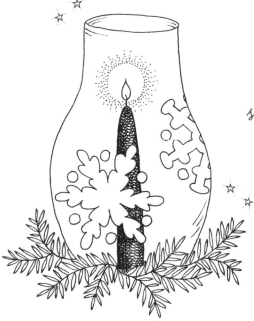

Add some wintry snowflakes to votive holders, canning jars or flower vases, too!

Christmas in the Country

Holiday Swags

Valerie Bryan
Woodbridge, CT

We live in a home built in 1753 and like to decorate with lots of natural items, like these easy-to-make greenery swags.

evergreen roping
medium-gauge wire
holly branches

pine cones
boxwood sprigs
wired ribbon

Cut roping to desired length, then use wire to attach holly, pine cones and boxwood along the roping. Using the wired ribbon, you can either make bows and wire them along the length of the evergreen, or wrap the ribbon around the entire length of the swag. Secure your greenery swag around the stair railing, over doors or along a porch railing.

Christmas Greenery

Diane Treichler
Attleboro, MA

A great way to use your trimmed branches.

evergreen branches
holly or winterberries
small red bows

When pruning your Christmas tree's bottom branches, rather than throwing them away, arrange the greenery on your dining room chandelier. Add a few holly berries, winterberries or small red bows and you'll have a beautiful and fragrant decoration for the season. It's so simple to make and looks wonderful!

Gone Fishin' Tree

Connie Mattison
Belmond, IA

This year decorate with a favorite theme!

lures
bobbers
white lights

fishing net
fishing cap
scrap plywood

Our son likes to fish, so one year I decided to decorate a fishing tree for his room. I emptied his tackle box and used lures and bobbers for ornaments, added white lights and I even found a string of lights with trout-shaped bulbs! A fishing net was added and his favorite fishing cap became the tree topper. From scrap plywood I painted a sign that said "Gone Fishin'" and hung it on the tree. It was the hit of the house!

Think of all your hobbies, choose a favorite and create a theme tree! Do you like gardening? Fill your tree with seed packets, miniature gardening tools, gloves and tiny terra cotta pots. Top it off with a brimmed straw hat!

Cheery Snowmen

Pam Ecton
Gridley, KS

*For years I've been making these snowmen as gifts for friends
and family...they're really easy!*

shredded paper
all-purpose flour
3 foam balls
toothpicks
twigs

orange paint
2 black beads
red paint
fabric scraps

Fill an old kettle with water; bring to a boil. Add shredded paper and
let simmer until paper begins to fall apart, usually about 30 minutes.
Stir occasionally to keep paper from sticking to kettle. Drain excess
water and use a hand mixer to break up paper. Add enough flour to
the mixture until you have a sticky dough consistency; set aside. Use
any size foam balls for your snowman body. So the snowman will
stand, cut a small portion off the bottom ball. Use toothpicks to hold
the 3 balls together and add a toothpick where you'll want each arm
to be. Mold the paper mixture around the balls
until they're well covered. Remove arm tooth
picks and insert small twigs, add an orange
painted toothpick for the nose. Let dry in a
warm place for several hours, then glue on
black beads for eyes and paint on rosy
cheeks. A hat can be made from a length
of fabric glued into a tube shape. Tie it at
one end with raffia and roll
the other; slip on your
snowman's head, tie on a
scarf and your snowman is
ready for the holidays!

*Christmas means a
spirit of love...*

-George McDougall

Canella Berry Tree

Dana Cunningham
Lafayette, LA

*Cheery canella berries are everywhere at Christmas. This year
we used them to make a beautiful canella berry tree!*

cone-shaped grapevine tree or
    wire tomato cage
hot glue gun and glue

canella berry branches
medium-gauge wire

Begin with a cone-shaped grapevine tree or a tomato cage. If you're
using a tomato cage, you'll need to clip the wires from the bottom to
make it stand evenly. Using a hot glue gun, glue branches of canella
berries to the grapevine or wire them to the cage. Continue to overlap
the canella berry branches until the cage or grapevine can't be seen
beneath. Tiny trees look pretty sitting on a dry sink or lined along the
center of a buffet table. Larger trees bring lots of color to a wintry
snow-covered garden.

*Oh! holly branch
and mistletoe,
and Christmas chimes
where 'ere we go,
and stockings pinned
up in a row! These are
thy gifts, December.*

-Harriet F. Blodgett

Christmas in the Country

Handmade Garland

Cheri Maxwell
Gulf Breeze, FL

Several years ago, our family settled into a log cabin nestled in the woods. We love being surrounded by tall evergreens and the quiet peace that seems to be everywhere. At Christmas, we try to keep our holiday decorations natural and simple.

heavy-gauge wire or length of homespun
heavy paper
scissors
quick rusting thin steel

hole punch
unbleached muslin
teabags
needle-nose pliers

Cut a length of wire or homespun the same length as your mantel. Draw several different shapes and sizes of stars on heavy paper, then cut them out to create patterns. Place each pattern on a sheet of thin steel made for quick rusting and cut shapes out with scissors. Add a hole in the top of each star for hanging, then follow the manufacturer's instructions for quickly rusting steel. After stitching together several small mittens from muslin, add a loop of thread for hanging. You can tea-dye mittens for an antique look. Just add a teabag to a cup of hot water and let steep. Remove the bag and dip your mitten in the tea until it's as dark as you'd like; let dry. Once the mittens are dry and the stars rusted, slip them onto the wire or homespun, alternating each. Use needle-nose pliers to make small loops on each end of the wire or tie bows on homespun so the garland can be secured to the mantel over a small nail.

...why this is Christmas day!

-David Grayson

Rusty Tin Decorations

Carol Bull
Delaware, OH

*Primitive tree decorations look wonderful on feather trees or
on a country-style tree filled with cranberry
garlands and homespun bows.*

rusty tin stars, hearts or sheets
   of quick-rusting steel
hole punch

medium-size jingle bells
medium-gauge wire
needle-nose pliers

If you can't find rusty hearts or stars, you can make your own by
purchasing lightweight steel at your local craft store that's especially
made to rust quickly and is easily cut with scissors. Follow the
manufacturer's instructions for rusting the steel, then punch a hole in
the top for hanging. If you'd like to rust your bells, rough their surface
with sandpaper and leave them in vinegar to rust. To make your
ornament, gently bend a 6 to 8-inch length of wire in an upside-down
"U" shape. Slip the hole in your star over one end of the wire then use
needle-nose pliers to gently twist the wire and secure the star. Place
the jingle bell on the other end of the wire and secure it also. Your
old-fashioned ornaments will look wonderful draped over the branches
of your Christmas tree.

*The whole world
is a Christmas tree,
and stars its
many candles.*

–Harriet Blodgett

Christmas in the Country

Star-Shaped Apple Ornaments

Connie Bryant
Topeka, KS

*Ever since I can remember, we've loved sprinkling stars throughout
our home during the holidays. Last year we made these
two ornaments to add to our collection.*

apples
star-shaped cookie cutter
lemon juice

coarse salt
homespun fabric
awl

Cut each apple crossways into several thin slices, then cut each slice
into a star with a star-shaped cookie cutter. Soak the slices in lemon
juice overnight to keep them from turning brown, then in the morning
remove them from the lemon juice and sprinkle with coarse salt. Place
the slices in a dehydrator to dry or on a baking sheet in a 200 degree
oven for 6 to 8 hours. Apple slices should be leathery to the touch
when completely dry. Use an awl to punch a small hole in the top of
your star, then slip a narrow length of homespun through the hole and
hang on the tree.

Cinnamon Stars

one-inch cinnamon sticks

medium-gauge wire

Small, one-inch cinnamon
sticks can be slipped over a length
of wire that's easily formed into
a star shape. Use needle-nose
pliers to twist ends together and
close star shape. Pile stars in a
yellowware bowl, toss in a basket
with evergreens and pine cones
or set in the individual panes of
your windows.

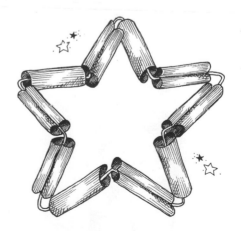

Tiny Trees

Linda Seidel
North Olmsted, OH

*Tiny potted trees are perfect accents for small
tables and country cupboards!*

tiny potted pine trees
burlap squares

small gravel
variety of small containers

Water your pine trees well, then use burlap squares to hide the pot
they're planted in. Fill your container 2/3 full with small gravel then
tuck in your tree. Use lots of old-fashioned containers such as an
antique sap bucket, teapot, redware pitcher, coffee pot, sugar bucket or
basket. Set your trees in places where you don't have a lot of room,
but would like some holiday cheer…small tables, a step-back
cupboard, mantel, blanket chest or trunk. After the holidays are over,
remove your tree from its pot and plant outside as a reminder of this
year's Christmas fun.

*Create a memorable
holiday centerpiece.
Fill a large, clear glass bowl
with several nostalgic photos
of past Christmases…kids
opening packages,
Mom baking cookies
or Dad hanging lights.
Be sure to place the photos
facing outward so they
can be seen, then fill the bowl
with lots of greenery
and ornaments.*

Christmas in the Country

Ice Candles

Nancy Stinson
Muncie, IN

*I grew up in a historic town and whenever we had a Christmas
candlelight walk, the sidewalks between the homes and
along the quaint shops would be lined with these.*

tall, narrow buckets
cranberries
holly leaves
pepperberries
evergreen sprigs

paper cup
pebbles
tape
votive or tea light

Fill any tall, narrow bucket with water; a sap bucket would be perfect.
Add lots of fresh cranberries, holly leaves, pepperberries or evergreen
sprigs to the water. Fill a paper cup with pebbles then stretch 4 or
5 strips of tape from the inside of the cup to the outside of the bucket.
Make tape strips long enough that they'll secure the cup in the middle
of the bucket to keep it from sinking to the bottom. Freeze until the
water's solid, slide off the bucket and remove the paper cup. You may
have to tear the cup out a little at a time to remove it completely, then
set a votive or tea light in the hole created.

*Ice candles can be made in
lots of different shapes. Use
a half-gallon milk carton
for a square candle,
or a plastic gallon jug for
a chubby round one!*

Pumpkin Snowman

Mary Mullen
Colleyville, TX

With three small children, every year we seem to end up with lots of uncarved pumpkins, so for several years I've been turning them into winter snowmen!

3 pumpkins
white acrylic paint
hot glue gun and glue
straight pins
black buttons
orange foam
hat

flannel scarf
metal hangers
felt squares
wire cutters
cardboard
cotton balls

Hot glue pumpkins together, beginning with the largest on the bottom and the smallest on top. Paint all 3 pumpkins with 2 or 3 coats of white acrylic paint; let dry between each coat. Using a glue gun or straight pins, attach black buttons for the eyes and mouth, then add buttons down the front of the snowman. Cut orange foam into the shape of a carrot and hot glue to the snowman, add a top hat and a flannel scarf. To make his arms, use metal hangers that have been cut with wire cutters and tuck them in the sides of the snowman. Using felt, cut out 4 mitten shapes, glue 2 sides together and slip the open ends over the wire arms. Bend a section of cardboard to resemble a pipe then add cotton balls so it looks like smoke is curling up and away from the pipe.

A grapevine wreath covered with dried, red cockscomb will make a beautiful holiday wreath!

Christmas in the Country

Blooming Centerpiece

Diana Chaney
Olathe, KS

These cheerful flowers are beautiful during winter's chill!

large twig basket
several canning jars
paperwhite bulbs
pebbles

pine cones
pomegranates
greenery sprigs
pomanders

We love to have friends and neighbors over each year for a holiday buffet. It's very casual; they drop by when they can and stay as long as they'd like. We have all the old familiar Christmas music playing, a crackling fire in the fireplace and lots of homemade goodies. I always pull the chairs away from our dining room table so there's extra seating and set out a variety of home-baked cookies, appetizers, spiced cider and eggnog. In the center of the table I set a large twig basket filled with several canning jars of paperwhite bulbs I've been forcing. If I begin forcing the bulbs in early November, they're blooming just in time for Christmas! To hide the canning jars, I surround them with pine cones, pomegranates, greenery sprigs and pomanders. If the paperwhites are very tall and need securing to stand upright, just tie them loosely together with several strands of raffia.

Legend has it that burning a bayberry candle on Christmas Eve brings good luck throughout the new year.

Heirloom Kitchen Tree

Elizabeth Blackstone
Racine, WI

A family heirloom becomes a sentimental holiday decoration.

sugar buckets
crumpled newspaper
Spanish moss

narrow tree branches
cinnamon ornaments
homespun fabric

I have a collection of old-fashioned sugar buckets that were handed down to me from my grandmother. Each one is a different color and they're not only pretty, but sentimental. I keep them stacked in my kitchen where I can always see them. The buckets remind me of spending time with my grandmother while I watched her make wonderful homemade bread and rolls. Each year when we decorate for Christmas, I always try to fit a tree in the kitchen, but there just isn't enough room. This year, however, we came up with a perfect solution.

I removed the lid from the top sugar bucket and packed it tightly with crumpled newspaper. To hide the newspaper, I covered it with Spanish moss. Then I cut several narrow tree branches that had lots of twisting vines and tucked them in the sugar bucket. For a family activity we made snowflake-shaped cinnamon ornaments and tied on scraps of homespun to hang them by. We slipped them over the branches and they were beautiful...a homespun and sentimental Christmas tree.

For Christmas is
tradition time...

—Helen Lowrie Marshall

Christmas in the Country

Memory Jars

Geneva Rogers
Gillette, WY

Display your favorite photos in a clever way!

color copies of photos   variety of glass bottles

Right before the holidays my husband's grandmother gave us a lot of very old family photos. Several of these family photos were just too wonderful to pack away…three sisters posing together in their flapper dresses, a young couple cutting their wedding cake and a little girl at the World's Fair. In a few short days our families would be coming to spend the holidays with us and I wanted to display the photos when we were all together. Finally I came up with an idea that worked out beautifully! To preserve the original photos, I made sepia tone copies of my favorites and slipped them into a variety of old-fashioned bottles…milk bottles of all sizes, old glass canning jars, cream-top bottles and small 1/2-pint canning jars. After gently rolling the photocopies, they easily slipped through the openings in the jars. I displayed the jars on the shelves of an open pie safe along with sprigs of greenery, old-fashioned sifters and graters. After everyone arrived, we had a wonderful day together sharing family memories.

Color copies of family photos also make heart-felt greeting cards. Cut copies out with decorative-edge scissors and write your holiday messages on the back!

Candle Ornaments

Jill Valentine
Jackson, TN

Give your holiday tree an old-fashioned look.

small votives
cinnamon
cloves
allspice

wax
double boiler
small paint brush
medium-gauge wire

After purchasing several small votives I decided I wanted to give them an antique look before using to decorate my tree. I added ground spices such as cinnamon, cloves and allspice to wax I had melted in a double boiler. I brushed the votives with the mixture and let cool. Then I laid a length of thin wire on the table and placed my votive in the middle, on its side. I brought each end of wire up and around the middle of the votive several times to secure it then made a loop from the wire for hanging. I slipped the wire loop over the tree branches, added other ornaments such as homespun bows, beeswax ornaments and a garland of cranberries for a wonderful, old-fashioned Christmas tree. For safety reasons, these candles should never be lit, they're simply to add a vintage feel to holiday decorations.

Sweet is the smile of home; the mutual look when hearts are sure of each other.

—John Keble

Handmade Gifts

Painted Kindling Bucket

Kelly Alderson
Erie, PA

*A handpainted holiday kindling bucket is a gift your neighbors
will be sure to enjoy on a chilly winter night!*

galvanized bucket
cotton cloth
vinegar
white primer
acrylic paint

paintbrush
antiquing medium
non-yellowing matte sealer
twigs, fatwood, dried herbs and
    fireplace matches

Wipe down the bucket with a cotton cloth saturated in vinegar; let dry.
Apply a white primer; let dry. Choose any pattern for your bucket or
use stencils and paint on a design with acrylic paint. When dry, fill a
paintbrush with a contrasting color paint and run your thumb over the
bristles to spatter paint over the bucket. Following the manufacturer's
instructions, cover the bucket with an antiquing medium and let dry.
Coat your bucket with a non-yellowing matte sealer to protect the
paint and let dry thoroughly. Fill your basket with twigs collected from
your yard and a bundle of fatwood tied
with raffia; these will make
wonderful firestarters. Bunches of
herbs tied together will give off a
sweet scent when tossed on a
fire and be sure to tuck in
some long fireplace matches
as well.

*Home, the spot of earth
supremely blest
a dearer, sweeter, spot
than all the rest.*

—Robert Montgomery

Handmade Gifts

Snow-Kissed Votives

Vickie

Easy-to-make frosted votives are a festive Christmas gift!

glass votive holders   votive candles
silver metallic permanent ink
    markers

Purchase glass votive holders, either clear or tinted, wash with soapy warm water and dry well. Use silver metallic permanent ink markers in different tip sizes to write holiday messages such as "Merry Christmas" and "Ho, Ho, Ho!" You can even use them to mark place settings, just personalize them with each guest's name! You can add designs such as snowflakes or snowmen or draw on party hats and write "Happy New Year" and tuck in a votive. These are just the right size to tuck in stockings or keep several in a basket by the door for quick gifts.

Wrap glass votives with strands of copper or gold wire. It's easy to find at hardware stores and adds a pretty sparkle to your table.

Handmade Soap

Laura Fuller
Ft. Wayne, IN

Wrap these up in vintage doilies and tie with a ribbon.

12-oz. unscented, white soap,
   grated
1 c. water
eye dropper
food dye

fragrance oil
freezer paper
heavy-duty plastic containers
rubber gloves

Place grated soap in a stainless steel saucepan. Over low heat, add water and stir until soap melts and mixture forms a paste. Remove from heat and use an eye dropper to add desired amount of food dye and fragrance. Let cool slightly and pour into plastic containers; set aside to harden. When soap is completely hard, slice into blocks, place on freezer paper and let dry out for one week. Grate blocks in a stainless steel bowl and add just enough water to moisten; stir and drain any excess water. Slip on rubber gloves, remove a handful of soap and form into a hard ball; repeat. Let soap balls dry on freezer paper, turning so they dry evenly, for about 2 weeks.

Give your homemade soaps nestled in a gift tin or piled in a handmade basket. Add a soft cotton wash cloth, bath salts and scented votives for a relaxing gift that will certainly be appreciated.

Handmade Gifts

Button-Box Gift Tags

Lynda Robson
Boston, MA

*Original holiday gift tags are simple to make
and each one will be unique.*

heavy stock colored paper
decorative-edge scissors
glue stick

buttons
ribbon

Using a variety of colored paper, cut out tags in any size using several
different styles of decorative-edge scissors. You can even layer the
colors in your gift tags. Just cut 2 identical tag shapes, making one a
little larger than the other. Center the smaller tag on top of the larger
one and glue together with a glue stick; both colors will show. Fold
your tag in half and glue on old-fashioned buttons. Add a length of
pretty ribbon for attaching to your package.

Hang a cheerful
holiday greeting!
Bend heavy wire in
letter shapes,
you could spell out
"joy" or "Noel",
then attach fresh
greenery sprigs to the
wire letters with
green florist's tape.
Add a loop then hang
your message!

Warm Thoughts Jar

Kathy Macchione
Upper Arlington, OH

I've recently moved to Ohio and look forward to spending the holidays with my sister and family. My mom, however, lives in New Jersey and since it's the first Christmas season in a long time that we won't be together, I wanted to share something with her to cheer her up, so I've made a "Warm Thoughts" jar for her.

glass jar with a wooden lid   paper strips
acrylic paints

I painted a snowman's face on a pretty jar with a wooden lid and on the front of the jar I added a label that says "Countdown 'till December 25th." During Thanksgiving all of the family gathered in Ohio jotted down memories, wishes for the new year and warm thoughts on 24 slips of paper. I tucked each slip inside the jar and will send it to Mom so she can read a thought from the heart each day leading up to Christmas.

The manner
of giving
is worth more
than the gift.

-Pierre Corneille

Handmade Gifts

Vintage Ornaments

Nikkole Kozlowski
Columbus, OH

This is a wonderful old-fashioned craft started by my great-grandmother. It's so easy and fun to make!

fabric scraps
foam balls, eggs, cones, bells,
   any shape or size
straight pins

craft beads
craft confetti
ric-rac
gold thread or ribbon

Cut fabric scraps to fit foam forms. Vintage-looking fabrics in solids or prints will give the ornaments a nostalgic feeling, or you can also decorate the form without fabric. Begin with a simple design, just slip a straight pin through a bead or confetti shape and insert the pin in the foam. If you're using fabric scraps, repeat along the edges of fabric to hold it in place. Pins can also be used to secure a length of ric rac or try making a star or snowflake design with your beads or confetti. To make a loop for hanging, tie a length of gold thread or ribbon in a loop; knot one end. Slip a beaded pin through the knot and push into the top of the ornament.

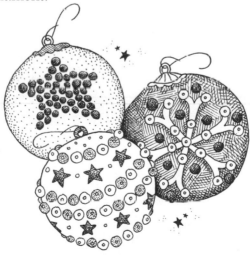

*Slip a flavored teabag or pressed flower
in with your holiday cards!*

Glowing Candles

Lynn Williams
Muncie, IN

*Each year we make a handcrafted gift to share with our friends
and this year we're sharing holiday candles.*

several glass containers
cinnamon sticks
lemon slices
cranberries
evergreen sprigs

rosehips
tiny pine cones
water
floating candles

For this gift, you can pack everything in a box and include the
instructions on how to make the candles or make and deliver them
at dusk. To begin you'll need to gather together several narrow glass
containers…canning jars, milk bottles, tumblers or juice glasses
will work. Loosely fill the jars with your favorite wintertime
decorations…cinnamon sticks, lemon slices, cranberries, evergreen
sprigs, rosehips or tiny pine cones. Add enough water to almost fill
the jar, then slip a floating candle on top. They're beautiful along
a mantel, or sit several different sizes in the middle of your dining
room table for a pretty centerpiece.

*Floating
candles are
also beautiful
in water-filled
custard cups.
They look so
pretty sitting
at individual
place settings.*

Handmade Gifts

Painted Flowerpots

Shari Cockerham
Seymour, IN

*Here's a great gift for teachers that you can enjoy making with
your kids. My daughter is 5 and we had a lot of fun
painting the flowerpots for her teachers.*

4-inch terra cotta flowerpot
white, red, black and yellow
   acrylic paint

matte sealer
Spanish moss

Paint the base of a 4-inch flowerpot red; let dry. Using white paint,
add the letters "A B C" or the words "Math" or "Science" over the
red paint. You could even paint a simple "1+1=2" math problem.
Then, paint the rim of the pot yellow and when it's dry, add black lines
and numbers so it resembles a ruler. When all the paint has dried
thoroughly, you can coat your flowerpot with a matte sealer to protect
the paint. When the sealer has dried, add Spanish moss in the bottom
and tuck in gifts a teacher would like such as pens, note pads, pencils
and some holiday candy.

*Give a friend who loves to
bake sweets a painted
flowerpot filled with
goodies for her
kitchen...oven mitts
and pot holders, sugar
jimmies, flavored baking
chips, cookie cutters and
a cake tester broom!*

Spicy Coffee Cozies

Donna Nowicki
Center City, MN

A warm, tangy aroma will fill the room whenever you set a hot mug on the mat!

4 cinnamon sticks, crushed	2 c. rice
2 T. whole cloves	2 7"x7" fabric squares

Combine cinnamon sticks, cloves and rice; set aside. Hem all edges of fabric and sew together on 3 sides. Scoop cinnamon mixture inside fabric and handstitch final side closed.

Frosty Friends

Ruth Naples
Mexico, ME

These darling snowmen are great as package tie-ons!

snowman cookie cutter	green floss
white and orange felt squares	polyester fiberfill
2 1/4-inch black pompons	red ribbon
3 1/2-inch black pompons	

Using your cookie cutter as a pattern, trace an outline on 2 squares of white felt; cut out. On one white cut-out, glue on two 1/4-inch pompons for eyes and three, 1/2-inch pompons for buttons. Cut a small carrot shape from the orange felt and glue on for snowman's nose. Pin both snowman shapes together, right sides out and blanket stitch around the outside edges with green floss. Leave an opening in the bottom, tuck in polyester fiberfill and then continue to stitch closed. Give your snowman a scarf by tying on a length of red ribbon.

Handmade Gifts

Snowy Day Bouquet

Megan Brooks
Antioch, TN

Enjoy the beauty of fresh flowers even during winter snowstorms!

containers
pebbles

variety of spring-blooming bulbs

Forcing bulbs is easy, you just trick them into thinking it's spring!
Hyacinths, paperwhites and amaryllis bulbs are easy to get started.
Choose a variety of bulbs without any blemishes, then gather several
different containers to grow them in...vintage milk bottles, canning
jars or spongeware bowls. Rinse and dry your container well; fill
3/4 full with pebbles. Set bulbs on gravel then add enough water to
cover gravel and cover the bottom half of the bulbs. Move the bulbs to
a sunny window, keep at room temperature and check the water level
weekly. The bottom half of the bulbs should always be covered with
water. Bulbs will bloom in 6 to 8 weeks.

Pack a gift box of springtime for a faraway friend! In a sturdy box, carefully wrap an oversize teacup, pebbles, several bulbs and directions for forcing the bulbs. It's wonderful to look forward to spring blossoms in winter!

Puffy Cinnamon Ornaments

Corrine Lane
Marysville, OH

These make the prettiest ornaments!

4 c. all-purpose flour
1/4 c. cinnamon
1 c. salt

3 T. nutmeg
2 T. cloves
1-1/2 c. lukewarm water

Sift together the flour, cinnamon, salt, nutmeg and cloves. Add enough water until the dough is the consistency of molding clay. Roll out to 1/8 to 1/4-inch thick and cut with cookie cutters. Insert a straw at the top if you'd like to string them for hanging on your tree or adding to packages. Bake at 300 degrees for one hour.

Scented Applesauce Ornaments

Mary Trunk
Frederick, MD

These ornaments are great for tying on packages or stringing together for a wonderfully scented garland.

1 c. cinnamon
1 T. cloves
1 T. nutmeg

3/4 c. applesauce
2 T. white glue
ribbon

Blend together cinnamon, cloves and nutmeg; stir in applesauce and glue. Knead dough until smooth, about 2 minutes. Divide dough into 4 portions and roll out each to 1/4-inch thickness. Cut with cookie cutters. If you'd like to hang them, insert a hole in the top with a straw. Place ornaments on racks or brown paper sacks to dry for several days. Turn daily so ornaments will dry evenly. Thread with ribbon for hanging.

Handmade Gifts

Bay Leaf Topiary

Penny Sherman
Cumming, GA

These tiny topiaries are perfect favors. Use them to mark each place setting, then guests can take them home to enjoy.

terra cotta pot
white paint
sandpaper
foam block
twig
foam cone

hot glue gun and glue
bay leaves
Spanish moss
tiny pine cones
snow spray

Paint a terra cotta pot with white paint. When the paint has completely dried, lightly sand some of the color off from around the edges and middle. Cut your block of foam to fit inside your terra cotta pot, trimming any excess. Push one end of the twig into the bottom of a foam cone for your tree trunk, then press the other end into the foam secured inside the pot. Using a glue gun and starting at the bottom of the cone, glue on the largest bay leaves. Work your way up the cone, layering on smaller bay leaves as you go up. Cover the foam in your terra cotta pot with Spanish moss, then top with tiny pine cones. If you'd like, you can add a little snow spray to your tree.

There's a dear old tree,
an evergreen tree,
and it blossoms once a year.
'Tis loaded with fruit
from top to root,
and it brings to all good cheer.

-Luella Wilson Smith

Homemade Suet Cakes

Jan Bowden
Big Prairie, OH

Wintertime gifts for your feathered friends!

2 c. creamy peanut butter
2 c. shortening
2 c. whole-wheat flour

8 c. cornmeal
wire suet feeder

In a saucepan, blend together peanut butter and shortening. Remove from heat and stir until well blended. Add flour and cornmeal until a dough forms. Turn dough on a wax paper-lined 13"x9" pan. Let stand until mixture cools and becomes stiff. Cut to fit inside your suet feeder and hang for the birds to enjoy!

Wintertime Bird Treats

Melody Taynor
Everett, WA

Quick to make, your birds will love these!

4 hamburger buns
mini cookie cutter
4 egg whites

birdseed
jute

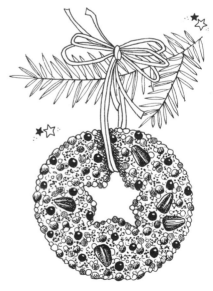

Slice each bun in half and remove the center with a mini cookie cutter. Beat egg whites until foamy; brush over insides of buns. Sprinkle on birdseed, pressing into place. Place the buns on a baking sheet and bake at 350 degrees for 10 minutes. Let cool then thread jute through the opening; hang on tree branches.

Handmade Gifts

Evergreen Wrapping Paper

Nancy Wise
Little Rock, AR

This makes absolutely beautiful giftwrap!

kraft paper
evergreen branches
newspaper

dark green paint
paint roller

Cover your work surface with a drop cloth, then lay kraft paper out flat. Weight down the paper edges to prevent curling. Place evergreen branches on a layer of newspaper and gently roll on a coat of green paint. Lightly press the evergreen branch on another layer of newspaper to remove excess paint. Gently press evergreen branch on the kraft paper, pressing needles onto paper to stamp on their outline. Repeat painting and pressing of evergreen branches over kraft paper until you have a design you like. If your branch and needles become too saturated with paint, begin painting with a fresh branch. Keep paper flat until completely dry.

Gather together pine cones in a variety of shapes, then glue each pine cone in a tiny terra cotta pot...perfect for each place setting!

Painted Gift Jars

Margaret Scoresby
Mount Vernon, OH

You can tuck all kinds of small gifts in this painted jar!

quart-size glass canning jar
spray paint
acrylic paint
paint brushes

stencil brushes
stencils
acrylic sealer

Wash a canning jar in warm, soapy water; rinse well and dry. Spray paint the outside the color of your choice; let dry. Paint or use stencils to add a design to the outside of your jar...snowflakes, evergreen trees, stars or a wreath. You could even sponge on lots of different colors; just be sure to cover all the glass so you can't see the inside. Let the paint dry thoroughly, then protect the paint with a coat of acrylic sealer. When the sealer is dry, tuck your gift inside...basic sewing supplies for a college student, a pair of woolen socks or mittens, cross-stitch patterns and a sampler of floss or hand-stitched bread cloths and your favorite bread recipe. Just tighten down the lid and tie on a homespun or raffia bow.

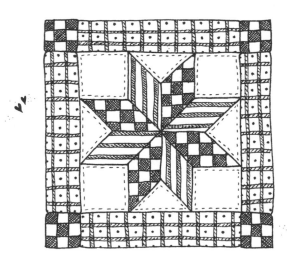

Handmade Gifts

Holiday Cornucopia

Liz Plotnick
Gooseberry Patch

*They're simple, quick to make and are a pretty change
from a holiday wreath. Great for hostess gifts.*

medium-gauge wire
twig cornucopia
evergreen sprigs

holly branches
magnolia leaves
ribbon

Create a hanger for the cornucopia by slipping a length of wire through the back of the cornucopia and making a loop; twist to tighten. Fill it with lots of greenery, holly, magnolia leaves and other winter favorites. Cut a long length of ribbon and tie a bow at the top of the wire hanger, leaving the ends of the ribbon quite long. Tuck the ribbon through the greenery branches then secure it at the bottom point of the cornucopia with a loose knot.

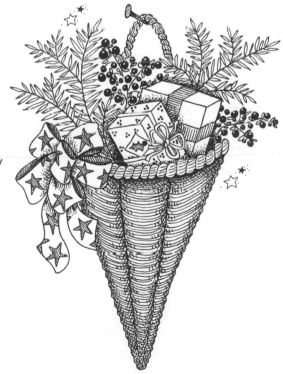

Bring back sweet childhood memories. Wire small children's toys...tiny airplanes, Teddy bears, dolls or toy trains on a cedar garland. Lightweight items can be hung from ribbon, heavier ones from floral wire.

Homespun Pins

Rita Morgan
Pueblo, CO

*These can be any size you'd like...simple to make
and perfect stocking stuffers!*

scrap paper	straight pins
unbleached muslin	floss in country colors
homespun fabric	hot glue gun and glue
pencil	teabag
batting	pin-back

Use scrap paper to sketch out a simple, primitive design...mittens, woolen stockings, feather tree or stars; set aside. Wash, dry and press your muslin and homespun before beginning, then decide what size you'd like your pin. Cut muslin and homespun to that size, adding a little extra for hemming. Tape your paper design to a bright window, lay your muslin over top and use a pencil to lightly transfer the design to your muslin. Layer your muslin over a square of batting cut the same size; pin together. Using 2 strands of floss, stitch over your design using a simple straight stitch. The more primitive and uneven, the better! When you're done, lay your muslin, stitched-side-down on a scrap of homespun cut the same size. Machine stitch around the edges, remember to leave an opening wide enough to turn the fabric right-side-out. Invert fabric then handstitch the opening closed. To "antique" the fabric, dip your teabag in a cup of hot water and let it steep until the water is as dark as you'd like. Let the water cool to lukewarm, then remove teabag and squeeze out excess water. Dab teabag over the muslin and stitching, making it as dark as you'd like. Let dry, then glue on pin-back.

Handmade Gifts

Gingerbread Wreath

Jane Ramicone
Berea, OH

Use all your favorite cookie cutters for this holiday wreath!

rust colored spray paint
18 inch metal wreath frame
cinnamon ornament dough

hot glue gun and glue
4 yds. ribbon

Spray paint metal frame; let dry. Prepare cinnamon ornaments according to recipe on page 178. Use cookie cutters to cut out your favorite shapes…gingerbread men, snowflakes, stars or hearts. When ornaments are dry, use hot glue to attach them to your metal wreath frame. Be sure to leave space at the top of the frame for your ribbon. When all the ornaments are securely glued on, slip the ribbon around the frame and tie into a bow.

Stuff a stocking with fresh greenery, princess pine and holly; a cheery greeting for your front door!

Keepsake Cookbook

Stephanie McAtee
Kansas City, MO

Create a book of memories to be shared and cherished.

recipe album
color copies of family photos
decorative-edge scissors
glue stick
collection of family stories

decorative paper punches
sheets of heavy cardstock
stickers
colorful pens
ruler

Too many times we wish we could prepare a favorite recipe we remember from childhood, but over the years the recipe's been lost or sometimes never even written down. This Christmas, make a keepsake cookbook that will be a treasured gift for someone you love. Be creative! Color copies of family pictures will really make your book special. Cut them out with decorative-edge scissors and scatter throughout your book. Take a tape recorder to family get-togethers and ask family members to talk about their best recipes and the story behind them, then write or type those memories next to the recipe. Sometimes heirloom recipes need adjusted to compensate for today's ingredients or ovens. You may even need to follow your mom or grandmother around the kitchen, take notes and measure the quantities as she cooks. Also, copies of handwritten recipe cards can add a sentimental touch to your book, so sprinkle them among typed recipes.

Candy Cane Hot Chocolate Mix

Mary Deaile
Fresno, CA

Yummy cocoa mix with a taste of peppermint...a cozy gift!

1-1/2 c. powdered sugar
1 c. plus 2 T. cocoa
1-1/2 c. non-dairy creamer

5 4-inch peppermint sticks,
   crushed
mini marshmallows

In a one-quart wide-mouth jar, layer powdered sugar then cocoa; packing each layer as tightly as possible. Wipe the inside of the jar with a paper towel to remove any excess cocoa before adding the next layer. Blend together non-dairy creamer and peppermint sticks, add to jar, packing tightly. Fill any remaining space in top of jar with a layer of mini marshmallows; secure lid. Before giving away, add the following instructions: Empty jar into a large mixing bowl; blend well. Spoon mixture back into canning jar. To serve, add 1/4 to 1/2 cup cocoa mixture to 3/4 cup boiling water; stir to blend. Makes 16 servings.

Thick blows my frosty
breath abroad;
and tree and house,
and hill and lake,
are frosted like
a wedding cake.

-Robert Louis Stevenson

Farmhouse Pantry

Brownie Sand Castles Mix

Wendy Paffenroth
Pine Island, NY

Who doesn't love brownies? This mix will be a welcome gift!

1/2 c. chopped pecans
1/2 c. semi-sweet chocolate
   chips
1/3 c. flaked coconut

2/3 c. brown sugar, packed
3/4 c. sugar
1/3 c. cocoa
1-1/2 c. all-purpose flour

In a one-quart wide-mouth glass canning jar, layer the first
6 ingredients in the order listed; packing each layer down well.
After adding the cocoa, use a paper towel to wipe the inside of the jar
to remove any cocoa from the sides; add flour. Cover filled jar with the
lid and tie on a gift card with the following instructions: Cream
together 2 eggs, 2/3 cup oil, one teaspoon vanilla extract and one
teaspoon almond extract. Stir in brownie mix and beat until well
blended. Spread batter into an oiled 8"x8" baking dish. Bake at
350 degrees for 30 to 40 minutes, or until the center tests done.
Cool on a wire rack. Makes approximately 1-1/2 dozen brownies.

Invite friends over and make your layered mixes "assembly line" style! You'll have more fun that way and everyone can catch up on each other's holiday plans!

Grandma's Noodle Soup Mix

Connie Hilty
Pearland, TX

*When a friend is feeling under the weather, they'll appreciate a
jar of this noodle soup mix. Quick to make, they
can enjoy it in no time at all.*

4 to 5 oz. fine egg noodles
3 T. chicken bouillon
salt and pepper to taste

1/2 t. dried thyme
1/2 t. celery seed
3 bay leaves

In a large mixing bowl, carefully blend together all ingredients. Add to
a one-quart wide-mouth canning jar; add lid. Tie on the following
cooking instructions: Combine noodle soup mix and 6 cups water in a
large stockpot. Add 3 carrots, diced, 2 celery stalks, chopped, and
one onion, chopped. Bring to a boil, reduce heat and simmer, covered,
for 20 minutes. Stir in 3 cups chicken and simmer 5 minutes longer.
Makes approximately 2 quarts soup.

Tuck your jar of noodle
soup in a basket with a
farmhouse bowl,
a loaf of freshly-baked
bread and sweet
creamy butter.
A warm-hearted
gift on a chilly
winter's day!

Farmhouse Pantry

Harvest Soup Mix

Regina Wickline
Pebble Beach, CA

Great to send in a care package to your kids away at college!

3/4 c. dried split peas
1/3 c. plus 2 T. beef bouillon
1/2 c. barley
3/4 c. dried lentils

1/2 c. dried, minced onion
3/4 c. long-grain wild rice
3/4 c. tiny bow tie or alphabet
    pasta

Blend together all ingredients and add to a one-quart wide-mouth canning jar; add lid. Tie on a gift card with the following instructions: Add soup mix to a large stockpot. Stir in 3 quarts of water, a 28-ounce can of diced tomatoes, undrained, and 1-1/2 pounds of stew beef, browned. Bring to a boil, then reduce heat and simmer, covered, for one to 2 hours, or until peas, lentils and rice are tender. Makes approximately 16 one-cup servings.

Jars of pantry mixes are perfect for college students!
Tucked inside a care package, they're sure to bring
a smile to someone who's missing Mom's cooking.

Ho-Ho Cocoa Mix

Kristie Rigo
Friedens, PA

*I like to tie a scoop onto the jar with raffia and give to
friends after a chilly afternoon of sledding!*

1-1/2 c. powdered sugar
1/2 c. cocoa
1-1/2 c. dry milk

1/2 c. non-dairy creamer
1-1/2 c. mini marshmallows

In a one-quart wide-mouth canning jar, add the powdered sugar,
packing down tightly. Layer cocoa, wiping the inside of the jar with a
paper towel to remove any excess cocoa. Stir together dry milk and
non-dairy creamer; layer over cocoa. Top jar with mini marshmallows;
add lid. Give the following directions: Blend together all cocoa layers in
a large mixing bowl; spoon back into canning jar. To serve, add 1/4 to
1/2 cup cocoa mix to 3/4 to one cup hot water. Makes 16 servings.

Fill a gift bag with a jar
of Ho-Ho Cocoa Mix,
chocolate-covered spoons,
a favorite holiday movie and
several bags of microwave
popcorn. Tie on a gift tag
that says "Let it snow!"

Farmhouse Pantry

Chocolate Chip Pie Mix

Kathy Grashoff
Ft Wayne, IN

A sweet, chocolatey treat!

1 c. sugar
1/2 c. all-purpose flour
6-oz. pkg. semi-sweet chocolate
    chips

1/2 c. flaked coconut
1/2 c. pecans, chopped

Blend together sugar and flour; place in a plastic zipping bag.
Seal bag and tie closed with a festive ribbon and tag that says "dry
ingredients." Combine chocolate chips, coconut and pecans in a
second plastic zipping bag and label "chocolate packet." Tuck both
in a holiday gift bag or decorated box. Add the following instructions:
Combine 1/4 cup butter, melted with dry ingredients. Add 2 eggs and
stir until dry ingredients are just moistened. Blend in chocolate packet,
then spoon mixture into a 9-inch pie crust. Bake at 350 degrees for
35 to 40 minutes.

*Home is where there's
one to love!
Home is where there's
one to love us.*

-Charles Swain

Fireside Coffee Mix

Lori Anderson
Eau Claire, WI

Give this mix as part of a gift bag with some chocolate-covered spoons or cinnamon sticks, freshly grated nutmeg and a can of whipped cream!

2 c. dry cocoa mix
2 c. non-dairy coffee creamer
1 c. instant coffee granules

2 t. cinnamon
1-1/2 c. sugar
2 t. nutmeg

Blend together all ingredients and place in an airtight container. Add these instructions for serving: For single serving, place 2 tablespoons of mix in a mug, add one cup boiling water; stir. Garnish with whipped cream and a sprinkle of nutmeg or cinnamon.

Hot Orange Cider Mix

Coralita Truax
Loudonville, OH

Add an orange or apple slice to each mug before serving.

1 c. sugar
2 6-inch cinnamon sticks

1 whole nutmeg

Combine sugar, cinnamon sticks and nutmeg. Place in a plastic-lined goodie bag. Add these instructions: Place 2 cups apple cider and 6 cups orange juice in a slow cooker; stir in cider mix. Turn slow cooker to high for 2 to 3 hours or until cider is heated through. Remove spices before serving.

Give your coffee or cider mix in a pretty jar tucked in a tall, narrow paper bag tied with red raffia.

Farmhouse Pantry

Patchwork Bean Soup Mix

Amy Butcher
Columbus, GA

This colorful soup mix would be great paired with crazy quilt potholders or oven mitts!

1/2 c. dried kidney beans
1/2 c. dried black-eyed peas
1/2 c. dried black beans
1/2 c. dried red beans
1/2 c. dried split green peas
1/2 c. dried Great Northern
   beans
1/2 c. dried kidney beans

1/2 c. dried lima beans
3 T. chicken bouillon
1 T. dried, minced onion
salt and pepper to taste
1/2 t. garlic powder
1 T. dried parsley flakes
1 t. celery seeds
1/4 c. brown sugar, packed

Layer 1/2 cup of each type of bean in a one-quart wide-mouth canning jar. In a plastic zipping bag, blend together seasonings. For gift giving, attach the following instructions: Add beans to a large stockpot, cover with hot water and let soak overnight. Drain and add 2 quarts of water. Bring to a boil, reduce heat and simmer, covered, one to 2 hours or until beans are almost tender. Stir in two, 14-1/2 ounce cans stewed tomatoes and seasoning mix. Simmer, uncovered, one to 1-1/2 hours or until beans are tender. Makes approximately 12 cups of soup.

Soup mixes don't need to be layered in a jar if you're short on time. Give the mix in a no-sew bag for an easy and welcome gift!

Jolly Gingerbread Men Mix

Kay Morrone
Des Moines, IA

Place a jar of this mix in a basket with a gingerbread man
cookie cutter...a wonderful gift for a secret pal!

3-1/2 c. all-purpose flour,
   divided
1 t. baking powder
1 t. baking soda

1 c. brown sugar, packed
2 t. ginger
1 t. cinnamon
1 t. allspice

Sift together 2 cups flour, baking powder and baking soda. Spoon into a one-quart wide-mouth canning jar, packing down tightly. Layer on brown sugar, pushing down well. Blend together remaining flour, ginger, cinnamon and allspice; layer over brown sugar and secure lid. Tie on the following instructions: Cream together one stick butter, 3/4 cup molasses and one egg, stir in dry mix; dough will be stiff. Cover and refrigerate one hour. Roll dough to 1/4-inch thickness on a lightly floured surface, adding additional flour if dough is too sticky. Cut with cookie cutters and place on a lightly oiled baking sheet. Bake at 350 degrees for 10 to 12 minutes. Makes 5 to 6 dozen cookies.

A snack attack basket is perfect for teenagers! Fill a colorful basket with mixed nuts, chocolate-covered pretzels, potato chips or caramels!

Farmhouse Pantry

Favorite Chocolate Chipper Mix

Robbye Shafer
San Antonio, TX

You can easily change the taste of this recipe by substituting white chocolate or butterscotch chips for the chocolate chips.

1/2 c. sugar
1/2 c. chopped pecans
1 c. semi-sweet chocolate chips
1 c. brown sugar, packed

2-1/2 c. all-purpose flour
1 t. baking soda
1/4 t. salt

In the order listed, layer the first 4 ingredients in a one-quart wide-mouth canning jar. Sift together the flour, baking soda and salt, add to canning jar; pack down tightly. Secure lid and tie on these directions: Cream together 3/4 cup butter, one egg and one teaspoon vanilla. Stir in dry ingredients; blending well. Shape dough into one-inch balls and place on a lightly oiled baking sheet. Bake at 350 degrees for 12 to 15 minutes. Makes approximately 3 dozen cookies.

Invite friends over for a "Trim the Tree" night! Turn on festive music and serve lots of yummy appetizers, sweets and punch. Give everyone a jar of your favorite pantry mix to say "Thanks for helping out!"

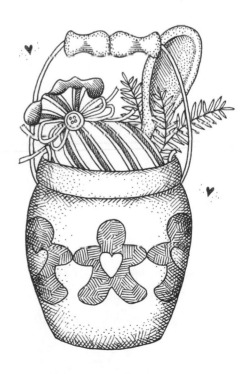

Chocolatey-Peanut Butter Cookie Mix

Kendall Hale
Lynn, MA

Two of my favorite flavors in one terrific cookie!

1 c. brown sugar, packed
1-1/2 c. powdered sugar
3/4 c. cocoa

1-1/2 c. all-purpose flour
1 t. baking powder
1/4 t. salt

In a one-quart wide-mouth canning jar, layer the first 2 ingredients, packing down as tightly as possible. Add cocoa, pack down, then wipe the inside of the jar with a paper towel to remove any excess cocoa from the sides. Sift together the flour, baking powder and salt, add to jar; pack down tightly. Attach a gift tag that reads: Cream together one stick butter, 2 eggs and 1/2 cup peanut butter; stir in dry mix. Shape into balls and place on a lightly oiled baking sheet. Bake at 350 degrees for 15 to 20 minutes. Makes approximately 2-1/2 to 3 dozen cookies.

A packet of gourmet cocoa tucked into a mug, cookie cutters with your favorite recipe attached, handmade ornaments or layered mixes are all quick gifts for friends who drop by.

Farmhouse Pantry

Brown Sugar Rounds Mix

Kerry Mayer
Denham Springs, LA

Delightful with a cup of chamomile tea.

2-1/2 c. all-purpose flour
1/2 t. baking soda
1/4 t. salt

1-1/4 c. brown sugar, packed
and divided
1/2 c. chopped pecans

In a large bowl, blend together flour, baking soda and salt. Divide mixture in half and press approximately 1-1/4 cups into the bottom of a one-quart wide-mouth canning jar. Press down firmly so all ingredients will fit inside. Measure out 1/2 cup plus 1/8 cup brown sugar and layer it over flour mixture; pack down well. Add pecans, then layer on remaining brown sugar, packing tightly. Top with remaining flour mixture, pressing down until mixture fits completely into jar. Add a gift tag with the following instructions: Beat together 1/2 cup shortening and 1/2 cup butter until creamy. Add in jar mixture, stirring with a spoon until well blended. Beat together one egg and one teaspoon vanilla extract; stir into flour mixture. Shape dough in two, 10-inch rolls. Wrap in wax paper and chill for 48 hours. When ready to bake, slice cookies 1/4-inch thick and place on an ungreased cookie sheet. Bake at 375 degrees for 10 minutes or until firm. Makes approximately 6 dozen cookies.

Make snow ice cream! Whip one cup heavy cream, stir in vanilla extract and sugar to taste, then add 4 cups of fresh, clean snow...so yummy!

Oatmeal-Raisin Cookie Mix

Marlene Darnell
Newport Beach, CA

Give some warm cookies with your cookie mix. A wax paper-lined vintage oatmeal box would be the perfect container to stack them in.

2 c. quick-cooking oatmeal, divided
1 c. brown sugar, packed and divided
1 c. raisins

1/2 c. sugar
1-1/2 c. all-purpose flour
1/4 t. baking soda
1 t. baking powder
1/2 t. cinnamon

Layer the following in order in a one-quart wide-mouth canning jar; pack each ingredient layer tightly. Add one cup oatmeal, top with 1/2 cup brown sugar; packing down tightly. Add raisins, then layer on remaining brown sugar, packing tightly. Layer on sugar, top with remaining oatmeal. Blend together flour, baking soda, baking powder and cinnamon until thoroughly combined. Add this mixture on top of the sugar layer, adding a little at a time, pressing down as you add. Secure jar lid and write the following instructions on your gift tag: Beat together 3/4 cup butter, 2 eggs and one teaspoon vanilla; blend in jar mix. Drop cookies by spoonfuls on an ungreased cookie sheet. Bake at 375 degrees for 10 to 12 minutes. Makes about 4 dozen.

Make a tape recording of your children singing Christmas carols together...it's a gift Grandma & Grandpa will treasure for years.

Farmhouse Pantry

Soft Drop Sugar Cookie Mix

Annette Ingram
Grand Rapids, MI

Friends will love receiving this easy-to-make drop sugar cookie mix!

4 c. all-purpose flour
1 t. baking powder
1/2 t. baking soda

1/2 t. salt
3/4 t. nutmeg
1-1/2 c. sugar

Sift together flour, baking powder, baking soda, salt and nutmeg
until thoroughly blended; add sugar. Spoon mixture into a one-quart
wide-mouth canning jar; pack firmly, jar will be tightly filled. Secure lid
and tie on the following instructions: Blend together one egg and one
cup butter; add 1/2 cup sour cream and one teaspoon vanilla. Stir in
dry ingredients from jar and chill dough overnight. Drop cookies by
spoonfuls on an ungreased cookie sheet. Bake at 375 degrees for
10 minutes or until lightly golden. Makes about 2 dozen.

*For a fun family present, have your parents'
old home movies transferred to easy-to-watch
video tapes; everyone will love reminiscing!*

Thumbprint Cookie Mix

Athena Colegrove
Big Springs, TX

An old-fashioned favorite...you'll love 'em!

3 c. all-purpose flour
2 c. sugar

1-1/2 c. chopped pecans

In a large bowl, blend together flour and sugar. Spoon into a one-quart wide-mouth canning jar, packing down tightly. Cut a circle of wax paper to fit just inside the canning jar; slip over the flour and sugar mixture. Lay the pecans over the wax paper; secure jar lid. Add the following instructions to your jar cookie mix: Cream together 1-1/3 cup butter, 4 egg yolks and 2 teaspoons vanilla until well blended. Open jar and remove pecans; set aside. Blend remaining jar mix with butter mixture. Cover and chill overnight. Whisk together 4 egg whites; set aside. Shape chilled dough into one-inch balls, roll in egg whites then in reserved pecans. Place on a lightly oiled baking sheet and press your thumb in the center of each cookie. Bake at 375 degrees for 10 to 12 minutes. After cookies have thoroughly cooled, spoon your favorite flavor of jam in the center of each cookie. Makes about 2 to 3 dozen cookies.

Bundle up the kids and take a ride to enjoy all the holiday lights...the kids can even wear their pajamas! Wrap up in cozy blankets, sing carols and enjoy a fun-filled evening together.

Christmas Memories Collection

Lynette Martin
East Liverpool, OH

I was fortunate to have my grandparents living next door while I was growing up, and each time I walked through the orchard toward their home, I eagerly anticipated a story. Gran's stories would always unfold as we worked or walked together, and one afternoon while we were snapping beans she told me of a December day many years ago. She was 16-years old and my Pap was 20. They were to be married on December 21st in a little ceremony at Holly Church. It was 1931 and the 21st came with a winter blast and a heavy snowstorm that made it difficult to travel. Although Pap and Gran were determined to make their appointment, in the end the snow won and they missed their meeting with the minister. However, as providence would have it, the minister passed them on the road. Both parties stopped and in the middle of the mountain road with snow up to their knees, Mel and Hattie were married; nothing fancy, just love and commitment. Not even a picture was taken, yet they were happy. Since then 66 years have passed and when it snows in December, I always remember the young couple standing in the middle of the road giving their love to each other.

Make a snowflake tablecloth! Cut out paper snowflakes, scatter them on a blue tablecloth, then cover them with a layer of tulle netting, which will keep the snowflakes from slipping off the table.

Christmas Memories Collection

Linda Haiby
Blaine, MN

Thanks to a great aunt who had the patience to teach me, I was crocheting long before I could write. Of course, the first doily I ever made looked more like a red thimble than a doily, but it was a start. When I learned my A-B-C's, I began writing and illustrating short stories and poetry, often making them into little homemade books. Then one year my Grandmother gave me THE Christmas gift, I couldn't have been more ecstatic! I was only 5 years old and THE gift was nothing more than a simple box with a bright red cover that was filled with assorted scraps of fabric, scissors and other craft supplies...to me it was a whole world of things to make. Grandma couldn't have given me a more special gift, it meant more to me than any doll, game or toy. I will never forget that gift, how special it was or how deeply it touched me. Every holiday season I think of that simple little gift and hope the gifts I make will touch the hearts of others the way those loving scraps touched mine.

A sewing kit is the perfect gift for a college student.
Filled with buttons, needles, spools of thread
and scissors, it's a gift that will be appreciated
again and again!

Natalie Giauque
Salt Lake City, UT

One year for Christmas we received the most beautiful package. It was wrapped in gold paper with a lovely bow, and we expected it to be full of treasures and delights. When my father opened the package, out came a hideous silver bowl! On each end of the bowl there were elk heads and antlers. As my mother wondered what she was going to do with it, my dad put it on his head, stood up and announced that he was Thor, Norse god of thunder. We all got a good laugh and the bowl was then dubbed the "Thor Helm" which we wore all during the holidays. Now each Christmas as the "Thor Helm" comes out of its box and makes its appearance, I realize it really was a beautiful package that created a wonderful family Christmas tradition.

A set of crocks can make clever places to store all your Christmas wrapping supplies. Filled with ribbon, tape, scissors, pens and gift tags; everything you need will be right at hand.

Christmas Memories Collection

Meg Veno
Glenmoore, PA

While growing up on a farm in Pennsylvania, I could hardly wait for our family's annual Christmas barn party! It was always held on December 23rd and all our family and friends were invited. My 4 brothers and sisters, our cousins and I would rehearse the Nativity play that we would perform. Dad would set up bales of hay all over the barn, we'd decorate, then act out the Nativity. That night provided enough Christmas spirit to last us the whole year through and created more memories than I can count. Unfortunately, when my brothers, sisters and I went away to college, the tradition ended. But now, as we are having our own families, we are thinking of reviving the tradition in the old barn. We all feel that it would be even more special now to share it with our own children. Here's to getting that old barn ready and creating new memories for the next generation!

Use cinnamon sticks to frame your favorite greeting cards. Cut foamboard and a sheet of heavy paper slightly larger than the greeting card. Glue paper to foamboard and then the greeting card to paper. Hot glue long cinnamon sticks on all four sides, letting the greeting card show through the middle.

Karen Spreng
Westlake, OH

When I was young, our family always attended an 11:00 p.m. church service on Christmas Eve. I can remember the church being so beautiful…candles flickered, the tree sparkled and the air was filled with glorious music. As a young nurse, I worked until 11:00 pm and I knew I wouldn't be able to attend the service with my family. But as a special favor, the dear night nurse would arrive 15 to 20 minutes early so that I could leave. I would drive to our church and usually arrive just in time to sing the last hymn. As this continued and became a yearly occurrence, my mother would always turn around and look for me, nurses still wore white then, so I wasn't hard to miss. I would slip into the pew next to her, she would hold my hand and together we'd lift our voices to sing "Silent Night." The church lights were so dim that it seemed the only light came from the candles and my mother's smile. Mom died a number of years ago and not a day goes by that I don't think of her. Now, with my loving husband and beautiful daughters, we have carried on that tradition of always holding hands at the candlelight service while singing "Silent Night." I know in my heart that Mom is singing with us, too.

Use needle-nose pliers to shape 18-gauge wire into a star, leaving some extra wire at the ends. Set the star securely in a pot filled with ivy. In time, the ivy will grow around the star…perfect for the plant lover on your gift list!

Christmas Memories Collection

Phyllis Peters
Three Rivers, MI

I have found that during my lifetime it isn't the size or value of a gift that is so very important. What really matters is that someone cared enough to show their love by giving you a treasured gift from their heart. I remember a necklace my little grandson selected for me one Christmas. It was a tiny red bird attached to a framed, oblong mirror, extended on a gold chain. He was so happy when I wore that particular gift and never failed to ask me, "Do you like it, Grandma?" Some 25 years later that necklace has a place with my valuables.

Stephanie McAtee
Kansas City, MO

Today we had our first snow of the season, which meant that a tradition in my husband's family would take place. Every year on the first snow, my mother-in-law makes homemade long johns! So we bundle up the kids and head to NaNa and Pa's! It's a lot of fun and a great excuse for the family to get together. I have yet to create my own family's first snow tradition, but one day I will. However, for now we look forward to homemade long johns!

Maybe Christmas, he thought, doesn't come from a store.
Maybe Christmas, perhaps, means a little bit more.

-Dr. Seuss

Rachel Keller
Bothell, WA

Coming from a big family, Christmas has always meant getting together with dozens of relatives and going to Grandma Teuscher's for Christmas Eve dinner. My favorite Christmas memory is the year a big windstorm hit our town and the power went out. After lighting candles we all gathered in front of the fire and each of us shared our favorite Christmas memories. That night there were four generations laughing and crying together about Christmases past...I will never forget the closeness we felt that night.

Deborah Patterson
Carmichael, CA

For 4 years after I turned 7, I begged my parents for a bicycle. There wasn't a lot of money for extras, so I always rode my friends' bikes and just kept wishing for a bike of my own. On Christmas day when I was 11, all the gifts were opened and again, no bike. My mother started breakfast, then asked me to please go outside and get the loaf of bread she had left inside the car trunk. Although I thought it was a strange request, I looked in the car trunk, and lo, and behold there was my bike! Of course, I knew I'd be sharing it with my four sisters, but it was the most beautiful bike in the world to me!

A collection of white votives look so pretty on a milk glass cake stand.

Christmas Memories Collection

Jo Baker
Litchfield, IL

I recall Christmas at Grandmother's farm, often snow-bound; it looked like a picture post card. How snug and warm we were around the wood burning stove while all outdoors was covered with a soft blanket of snow. Then, off we would go to gather the most perfect balsam tree we could find on Grandmother's farm! We returned to the house for large cups of hot cocoa, scarcely able to wait until we could begin decorating the tree. My sister and I made large garlands of paper chains, and having saved every scrap of tin foil, we made lovely stars for the tree. We strung strands of popcorn, then used a box of Mother's washing powder whipped with water to simulate snow. There never was a prettier tree.

Elaine Goldberg
Ocean City, NJ

As I think back many years ago on a special Christmas Eve, I was certainly behind schedule with all the holiday preparations. We had a 6-week old baby boy, and as most first-time moms, the house was a mess, the presents unwrapped and the tree wasn't decorated. Much to my surprise my entire family and several friends descended upon our home that evening and brought gifts and lots of food. They helped me with the baby, we decorated the tree and wrapped all the presents! We had a great Christmas Eve gathering that year, and what began as an overwhelming day ended with wonderful memories of family and friends. That very impromptu party became the first of 23 yearly Christmas Eve gatherings to date. It taught me that even the unplanned and certainly disorganized, can turn into a memorable lifelong tradition.

Victoria Green
Cleveland, TN

Each year our parents tried to make Christmas very special. One year when my sister, Sonya, was 5 and I was 8, my parents made an audio tape recording of Santa entering our home and leaving gifts. My father changed his voice to sound like Santa's and as he entered through the front door he was talking to Rudolph about what presents we had asked for. As our dog barked, "Santa" left our gifts and enjoyed a slice of German chocolate cake, all the while ho, ho, ho-ing the entire 15 minutes of tape! Many years later we still enjoy listening to that tape. Now that we have families of our own, we try to come up with ideas to make our children's Christmases just as special, but this memory is a hard one to top!

Dip several pine cones into white semi-gloss latex or enamel paint; set them on wax paper to dry. Tossed into a basket or hung from your tree, they look like they've been dusted with snow.

Christmas Memories Collection

Tammy Kobza
Fremont, NE

When I was growing up, Christmas was always a special time that our entire community looked forward to. For weeks, our small country school worked hard at preparing the annual Christmas program. It meant memorizing lines to skits and practicing music. We would cut and glue construction paper garlands, then go home with glittery cheeks as we made our homemade decorations that would serve to create the Christmas mood. Moms spent many hours sewing costumes and dads…well they just came and enjoyed the production. Although every year holds sweet memories for me, one year in particular stands out. It was the year my sister and her classmate opened the production. As I remember it, they were the youngest so they would be the first on stage to welcome everyone and to recite a short poem. The poem was written such that each girl had a line, then the other responded and it would go back and forth until the poem's conclusion. The school was packed, the lights were turned down and butterflies were in our stomachs! We could hear my sister and her friend tip-toeing out onto center stage. The teacher hushed all of us backstage and pulled the curtain. As the curtain was drawn everyone could see that the two girls were in shock. Then suddenly, one of the girls blurted out "You go first!" then the other immediately said, "No! You go first!" The banter continued once, maybe twice and as the audience caught on to what was happening, laughter filled the school house! In the meanwhile, our teacher was frantically trying to coach the girls from backstage. While I don't remember how the opening blunder was handled, I do remember the show went on and for quite some time thereafter, it was my sister's opening act that was fondly remembered.

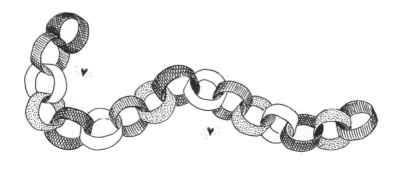

*Christie Paul
Knoxville, TN*

I remember one particular Christmas that made an indelible imprint on my life. I was 4 years old and my baby sister was one. I woke up early that morning to see all the presents, but noticed right away two new, fluffy Teddy bears. Mom and Dad announced that the bright, pink bear was for me and the brown one was for my sister, Amy. I was crushed. I was sobbing a little when I told Mom, "But, I wanted the chocolate Teddy bear not the strawberry one!" I'm pretty sure this is when I discovered my passion for chocolate!

*Sarah Beals
Halifax, MA*

Each year, as little girls, we would host a "Dolls' Christmas" in honor of Tasha Tudor's book. Each of our young friends would come dressed in their Sunday best and bring along their favorite doll dressed in the same manner. We would exchange doll-size gifts and would enjoy treats. Mom would read us "The Dolls' Christmas" and we would sing our favorite Christmas carols. Now I have two daughters of my own and I'm continuing this tradition with them. It has already become a great source of excitement for my girls as the holidays draw near each year.

*Host a progressive dinner this year.
It's fun to enjoy everyone's holiday decorations
and sample their cooking, too!*

Christmas Memories Collection

Sonia Schork
Lakeside, AZ

When I was approaching young womanhood in the late 1940's, I was obsessed with makeup! Oh, to be able to wear red lipstick, to powder my face, wear rouge and the forbidden of forbidden…mascara and eye shadow. But, my mother wasn't about to let me wear makeup in the eighth grade. I was to be content, alone seated at my dressing table, practicing for nothing and no one. The little box that I had of my mother's old makeup was only for my stuffed animals and dolls to see. When it was nearing Christmas 1946, I was the only girl in my class that still wasn't allowed to wear makeup and I felt like life was passing me by. On Christmas morning, I opened my gifts, my sweaters, pleated skirts and my new scatter pin sets. But, what I wanted simply wasn't there. I'd be without makeup for another year…how perfectly embarrassing! But then my mom said, "Did you look in your stocking?" I hadn't, but it was always the same…nuts, apples and a candy bar. But as I looked, there in the toe was a beautiful little box, done up prettier than all the rest. I opened it and there it was, a golden case of lipstick! I pulled off the top, it was mauve, not red, but by golly, it was lipstick! Then a horrible fear hit and I timidly asked, "May I wear it to school?" "Of course, you can, dear. You're old enough now."
I was struck with delight, overcome with more emotion than I can describe. I was grown up, a lady, maybe I could even go on a date! It was one of the most wonderful moments of my entire life! Later, as Mom showed me how to apply my mauve lipstick and blot it on a tissue so it wouldn't run, I flung my arms around her and cried with joy!

Alphabet-shaped cookie cutters are a quick way to share a holiday message. Set them along your mantel, cupboard shelf or windowsill!

Marilyn Behe
Little Falls, NY

When I was a little girl, every Christmas Santa put a big round orange in the bottom of our stockings. It always reminded me to be thankful for our many blessings. During the year, my mom would tell us about her Christmases. Sometimes the only gift that they would get would be a big orange in their stocking; Mom always said it was a treat to receive that orange in those days. To this day, my children receive that special orange in the bottom of their stockings. It reminds us to be thankful for everything that we have.

Whole dried oranges are so easy to make! Just cut several vertical slits through the orange peel, then place them on a rack in a 200 degree oven overnight. In the morning, place the rack of oranges in a dry spot so they can sit for one to two weeks, or until they're lightweight and very hard.

Christmas Memories Collection

Janice Leffew
Seattle, WA

My grandparents had a farm in Indiana and during the year the grandchildren would take turns visiting them. Each of the visits held its own share of fun and excitement, but lucky was the grandchild who visited in early December. I was 5 the first time this honor fell upon me, I hardly slept the week before my visit and my suitcase was packed almost as long! Finally the day came for Mom to take me to the farm. Snow had fallen and the gooseberry bushes that lined the lane were now covered with tiny, gleaming icicles; the effect was magical. After I unpacked my bags, the fun began! Grandpa arranged the multicolor lights on the tree while Grandma and I put candles on the windowsills. After Grandpa was finished, Grandma added the shiny balls of gold, red, blue and green, as well as the silver garland. Then it was my turn. I got to hang the tinsel. At first I was very careful to do it neatly. But then, as I got tired and the tree seemed to grow taller, I started throwing the tinsel at the upper branches. It looked messy to me, until Grandpa turned on the tree lights. Suddenly the tree was beautiful, as it glowed and shimmered. Later, during that weekend, Grandma made fudge. I kept busy making bell and star ornaments out of foil and cardboard as she worked, but this came to a halt as soon as there were pans to lick! When it was time to cut the fudge and pack it into the holiday tins, Grandpa made his appearance, sampled the fudge and announced it was even better than last year's. Now everything was ready, except for the gifts that they still had to make; Grandma at her sewing machine and Grandpa in his workshop. I couldn't stay to help them with this. It was time for me to return to the city, but that Christmas would become one of my favorite childhood memories.

Kari Swenson
Minnetonka, MN

When my cousins and I were little, someone made red elf hats for all eight of us. We would wear them Christmas Eve while we opened presents and played. It's a simple tradition, yet the memories and pictures are precious! Now as a second generation carries on the tradition, there are thirteen hats. Each year as our families gather, we read the Christmas story aloud and open presents. In that time, everyone is brought together and our thoughts are centered where they should be.

Leekay Bennett
Delaware, OH

Early into my marriage, over 30 years ago, I learned that becoming a military family meant constantly making new friends and saying goodbye to old ones. I wanted to remember those friends for years to come, so I designed a holiday memory tree. As the holiday parties began, families invited to our home were asked to bring one favorite ornament. As each guest arrived, I would write their name and the date on the ornament. I explained that each ornament on the tree held a special memory of friendship and that each family who brought an ornament to share, could choose an ornament of ours from the tree to take home with them as a reminder of the evening. Each year it was so much fun to open the memory box of ornaments and to remember our friends, wherever they were.

Christmas Memories Collection

Cyndy Sardeson
Ankeny, IA

There were many certainties about our big family gathering at Grandma's house on Christmas Eve, the kind of things that become part of a family's collective memory. We always knew that there would be a wonderful turkey feast, that Santa Claus would arrive at Grandma's front door sometime during the singing of "Jingle Bells" and that somewhere under Grandma's little Christmas tree there would be a box of small, flat and neatly wrapped packages. Everyone received one of those packages and we always knew what we'd find in them…a dollar bill and one of Grandma's special handmade hankies. The dollar bills are long gone, their use forgotten. But the hankies have endured the passage of time and have become treasured keepsakes. The worst thing we could ever say to Grandma would be to pronounce her hankies too pretty to be used. Gram was a practical, thrifty person who believed useful things should be used. I made sure she knew I definitely used most of my hankies and that I saved just a few of them for unknown special events that might occur in my future. I believe that it would please Grandma to know that my daughter as well as my daughters-in-law have each carried one of her special hankies in their bridal bouquets. She would also appreciate the fact that my granddaughter, the first arrival of the next generation, received my baby ring wrapped in one of those hankies on the day of her birth. One of these days, I'll be telling her the story of great-great grandma's Christmas hankies. When our lives get a little hectic and crazy during the holidays, we should stop and take a moment to realize that sometimes it's the simplest gifts that become the greatest treasures of our lives.

Fragrant oranges, apples and greenery bring the holidays to mind. Piled on an antique scale, they'll look right at home in your kitchen.

Index

Index

Index

Happy Christmas
to all, and to all
a good night!

—Clement Clarke Moore

We've cooked up a whole collection of Gooseberry Patch® books!

Have a taste for more? Call us toll-free at

1-800-854-6673

We'll send you our latest catalog filled with snowmen, Santas, ornaments, candles, cookie cutters, gourmet goodies, salt-glazed pottery collectibles and MORE...including our best-selling cookbooks!

Phone us:
1·800·854·6673

Fax us:
1·740·363·7225

Visit our website:
gooseberrypatch.com

Send us your favorite recipe!

and the memory that makes it special for you!* If we select your recipe for a brand new **Gooseberry Patch** cookbook, your name will appear right along with it...and you'll receive a FREE copy of the book! Mail to:

Vickie & Jo Ann
Gooseberry Patch, Dept. BOOK
P.O. Box 190
Delaware, Ohio 43015

*Please include the number of servings and all other necessary information!

fruitcake crocks Grandma's cookie cutters

orange pomanders cloves butter churn rolling pins

nutmeg gingerbread sprinkles dough bowls homemade bread

cinnamon vintage bowls sugar cookies